EDITOR: Maryanne Blacker
FOOD EDITOR: Pamela Clark

■ ■ ■

ART DIRECTOR: Sue de Guingand
ARTIST: Annemarlene Hissink

■ ■ ■

ASSISTANT FOOD EDITORS: Kathy McGarry,
Louise Patniotis
ASSOCIATE FOOD EDITORS: Karen Hammial, Lucy
Kelly, Enid Morrison
SENIOR HOME ECONOMIST: Justin Kerr
HOME ECONOMISTS: Emma Braz, Janene Brooks, Nadia
Kretchmer, Maria Sampsonis, Jodie Tilse, Amal Webster,
Lovoni Welch
EDITORIAL COORDINATOR: Elizabeth Hooper
KITCHEN ASSISTANT: Amy Wong
STYLISTS: Marie-Helene Clauzon, Carolyn Fienberg, Kay
Francis, Jane Hann, Cherise Koch, Sophia Young
PHOTOGRAPHERS: Robert Clark, Robert Taylor

■ ■ ■

HOME LIBRARY STAFF
ASSISTANT EDITORS:
Mary-Anne Danaher, Lynne Testoni
EDITORIAL COORDINATOR: Lee Stephenson

■ ■ ■

CIRCULATION & MARKETING DIRECTOR:
Chris Gibson
PUBLISHER/MANAGING DIRECTOR: Colin Morrison
CHIEF EXECUTIVE OFFICER: Richard Walsh

■ ■ ■

Produced by The Australian Women's Weekly Home Library.
Colour separations by ACP Colour Graphics Pty Ltd., Sydney.
Printing by Hannanprint, Sydney.
Published by ACP Publishing Pty. Limited,
54 Park Street, Sydney.
◆ AUSTRALIA: Distributed by Network Distribution
Company, 54 Park Street Sydney, (02) 9282 8777.
◆ UNITED KINGDOM: Distributed in the U.K. by Australian
Consolidated Press (UK) Ltd, 20 Galowhill Rd, Brackmills,
Northampton NN4 7EE (01604) 760 456.
◆ CANADA: Distributed in Canada by Whitecap Books Ltd,
351 Lynn Ave, North Vancouver B.C. V7J 2C4 (604) 980 9852.
◆ NEW ZEALAND: Distributed in New Zealand by Netlink
Distribution Company, 17B Hargreaves St, Level 5,
College Hill, Auckland 1 (9) 302 7616.
◆ SOUTH AFRICA: Distributed in South Africa by Intermag,
PO Box 57394, Springfield 2137, Johannesburg (011) 491 7534.

■ ■ ■

Sweet Temptations
Includes index.
ISBN 1 86396 053 8

1.Desserts. Title: Australian Women's
Weekly. (Series: Australian Women's
Weekly Home Library).

641.86

■ ■ ■

© A C P Publishing Pty. Limited 1996
ACN 053 273 546
◆ This publication is copyright. No part of it may be
reproduced or transmitted in any form without the
written permission of the publishers.

■ ■ ■

COVER: Chocolate-Brownie Caramel Tart, page 104.
Cake stand from H.A.G. Imports.
OPPOSITE: Passionfruit Liqueur Souffles, page 43.
Setting from Villeroy & Boch.
BACK COVER: Nectarine Ice-Cream Cakes, page 53.
Setting from The Bay Tree Kitchen Shop.

■ ■ ■

SWEET TEMPTATIONS

There is nothing quite as special or as fulfilling as indulging your sweet-tooth at the end of a meal. In this delightful cookbook, you will find some wonderful and inspiring recipes using the freshest produce from each season. Some of the recipes are quick and easy, some require more preparation, but all are delicious. Step-by-step photos will help newer cooks with some of the different methods, and our techniques section on page 124 also assists the novice.

Pamela Clark

FOOD EDITOR

BRITISH & NORTH AMERICAN READERS: Please note that
Australian cup and spoon measurements are metric. A quick conversion
guide appears on page 127.
A glossary explaining unfamiliar terms and ingredients appears on page 120.

Spring

As deliciously suggestive and imaginative as the promise of the season itself, this selection of luscious recipes is just right for spring. Best-of-the-seasonal fruits make an appearance in a minted passionfruit and pineapple sorbet and the grape gelato, while a hazelnut nougat ice-cream and warm mango galette will dazzle the palate of every sweetlover.

MANGO MERINGUE NESTS

3 egg whites
3/4 cup (165g) caster sugar
pinch cream of tartar

STRAWBERRY SAUCE
125g strawberries
2 tablespoons icing sugar mixture, approximately

MANGO CREAM
1½ medium (645g) mangoes
¼ cup (40g) icing sugar mixture
½ cup (125g) mascarpone cheese
125g packet cream cheese
¼ cup (60ml) cream
2 tablespoons caster sugar
3 teaspoons Malibu

Cover 2 greased oven trays with baking paper, mark 3 x 10cm circles 6cm apart on each tray. Beat egg whites in small bowl with electric mixer until soft peaks form. Gradually add sugar, beating until dissolved between additions. Gently fold in sifted cream of tartar.

Divide meringue among the 6 circles, use a spatula to make nest shapes. Bake in very slow oven about 1¼ hours or until nests are dry. Turn oven off, cool nests in oven with door ajar. Pour strawberry sauce and reserved mango puree (see Mango Cream) onto individual plates.

Gently press in centres of nests to make room for filling. Place nests on plates, fill with mango cream.

Strawberry Sauce: Push berries through strainer; discard the seeds. Sweeten to taste with icing sugar.
Mango Cream: Process mango flesh with icing sugar until smooth, strain. Measure 1/3 cup (80ml) puree for filling, reserve the remaining puree. Beat cheeses, cream and caster sugar in small bowl with electric mixer until smooth; stir in the 1/3 cup (80ml) mango puree and Malibu.

Serves 6.

■ Meringue nests can be made 1 week ahead. Strawberry sauce can be made a day ahead.
■ Storage: Unfilled nests, in airtight container. Strawberry sauce, covered, in refrigerator.
■ Freeze: Strawberry sauce and mango puree suitable.
■ Microwave: Not suitable.

CHOCOLATE PANFORTE WITH MAPLE SYRUP ICE-CREAM

The panforte is rich and should be served in thin wedges. Leftover panforte can be stored in an airtight container for several months.

2 sheets (15.5cm x 23.5cm) rice paper
1 cup (150g) plain flour
¼ cup (25g) cocoa powder
½ teaspoon ground nutmeg
¼ teaspoon ground cloves
1 teaspoon ground cinnamon
⅔ cup (130g) chopped dried figs
⅔ cup (100g) chopped dried peaches
1 cup (250g) chopped glace apricots
1⅓ cups (200g) raw hazelnuts, toasted
1⅓ cups (200g) raw cashews, toasted
½ cup (125ml) honey
½ cup (110g) caster sugar
½ cup (100g) firmly packed brown sugar
2 tablespoons water
150g dark chocolate, melted

MAPLE SYRUP ICE-CREAM
2 cups (500ml) milk
3 cinnamon sticks
8 egg yolks
1 tablespoon caster sugar
1 cup (250ml) maple-flavoured syrup
1½ cups (375ml) thickened cream

Grease deep 23cm round cake pan, cover base and side with 2 layers of baking paper. Cut rice paper sheets to fit base of pan.

Sift flour, cocoa and spices into large bowl; mix in fruit and nuts. Combine honey, sugars and water in small pan, stir over heat, without boiling, until sugar is dissolved. Simmer, uncovered, without stirring, 3 minutes. Pour hot sugar syrup then chocolate over nut mixture; mix well. Press mixture firmly into prepared pan. Bake in moderately slow oven 1 hour. Cool in pan.

Remove panforte from pan; wrap in foil, stand overnight. Serve thin wedges of panforte dusted with a little sifted icing sugar. Serve with maple syrup ice-cream.

Maple Syrup Ice-Cream: Combine milk and cinnamon sticks in large pan, bring to boil, remove from heat, stand for 5 minutes; discard cinnamon sticks. Whisk egg yolks and sugar in small bowl until thick and creamy, whisk in maple syrup. Gradually whisk egg yolk mixture into hot milk mixture, stir over heat, without boiling, about 15 minutes or until mixture thickens slightly. Transfer mixture to large bowl, press plastic wrap over surface of custard; cool. Refrigerate custard until cold.

Stir cream into custard, pour into deep 23cm square cake pan, cover with foil, freeze 3 hours or until just firm. Beat ice-cream in large bowl with an electric mixer until smooth. Return ice-cream to pan, cover; freeze until firm.

Serves 8.

■ Panforte can be made 3 months ahead. Ice-cream can be made 3 days ahead.
■ Storage: Panforte, in airtight container. Ice-cream, covered, in freezer.
■ Freeze: Panforte not suitable.
■ Microwave: Chocolate suitable.

Plates and spoon from Villeroy & Boch; gold tassel from Sirocco Homewares

WHITE-CHOC MOUSSES WITH MACADAMIA SHORTBREAD

Peach-flavoured liqueur or brandy could be substituted for the peach schnapps. An apricot-flavoured liqueur would also work well in this recipe.

3 eggs, separated
40g butter, chopped
1⅓ cups (200g) white chocolate
   Melts, melted
300ml thickened cream
2 tablespoons peach schnapps

MACADAMIA SHORTBREAD
¾ cup (105g) plain flour
60g cold butter, chopped
2 tablespoons caster sugar
2 egg yolks
½ cup (75g) macadamia nuts,
   toasted, chopped
⅓ cup (50g) white chocolate
   Melts, melted

Combine egg yolks and butter in medium bowl, stir over pan of simmering water until butter is melted. Whisk in chocolate; cool to room temperature.

Beat egg whites in bowl with electric mixer until soft peaks form. Fold egg whites, whipped cream and schnapps into chocolate mixture in 2 batches. Spoon into 8 x ⅓ cup (80ml) dishes, cover, refrigerate 3 hours or overnight. Serve with macadamia shortbread.

Macadamia Shortbread: Sift flour into bowl, rub in butter, stir in sugar, egg yolks and ⅓ cup (50g) of the nuts, mix to a soft dough, knead on lightly floured surface until smooth. Roll dough between sheets of baking paper until 3mm thick. Cut 32 x 3cm rounds from dough, place rounds 2cm apart on greased oven trays, sprinkle with remaining nuts. Bake in moderate oven for about 10 minutes or until lightly browned. Stand 5 minutes before cooling on wire rack; drizzle with chocolate.

Serves 8.

- White chocolate mousses best made a day ahead. Macadamia shortbread best made on day of serving.
- Storage: Mousses, covered, in refrigerator. Shortbread, in airtight container.
- Freeze: Not suitable.
- Microwave: Chocolate suitable.

Fabric from St James Furnishings; spoons from Mosman Antique Centre; tray from Corso De' Fiori

Spread chocolate evenly onto paper, stand until almost set.

Wrap collar gently around cheesecake. Stand until chocolate is set before peeling off paper.

Melt leftover chocolate. Spread onto marble slab, stand until set. Drag an ice-cream scoop along chocolate to form curls. Re-melt remaining chocolate and repeat process, if desired.

Serves 10 to 12.

- Cheesecake best made a day ahead. Chocolate collar and curls can be made 3 hours before serving.
- Storage: Cheesecake, covered, in refrigerator.
- Freeze: Not suitable.
- Microwave: Butter, marmalade, gelatine and chocolate suitable.

ABOVE: Chocolate Marmalade Baked Cheesecake.
RIGHT: Hazelnut Nougat Ice-Cream Terrine.

Glass cake stand from H.A.G. Imports; cake knife from Victoria Spring Designs

CHOCOLATE MARMALADE BAKED CHEESECAKE

200g packet plain uniced chocolate biscuits, finely crushed
100g butter, melted
1/4 cup (20g) coconut
3/4 cup (180ml) orange marmalade
2 teaspoons gelatine
1 tablespoon water

FILLING
2 x 250g packets cream cheese
3/4 cup (180g) mascarpone cheese
1/4 cup (55g) caster sugar
3 eggs
1 teaspoon grated orange rind
100g dark chocolate, finely chopped
1/2 cup (125ml) orange marmalade

CHOCOLATE COLLAR AND CURLS
2 cups (300g) dark chocolate Melts, melted

Grease 22cm springform tin, cover base with baking paper. Combine biscuit crumbs, butter and coconut, in large bowl. Press mixture over base of prepared tin, cover, refrigerate 1 hour.

Place tin on oven tray, pour filling into crumb crust. Bake in moderately slow oven about 55 minutes or until filling is firm. Cool in oven with door ajar. Cover cheesecake, refrigerate 3 hours or until cheesecake is cold.

Place marmalade in small pan, stir over heat until melted. Strain marmalade through fine strainer, into small bowl; discard rind.

Sprinkle gelatine over water in cup, stand in pan of simmering water, stir until dissolved. Stir gelatine through marmalade; stand 10 minutes. Pour marmalade mixture over cheesecake, smooth surface, refrigerate 1 hour or until glaze is set. Remove cheesecake from tin. Decorate cheesecake with chocolate collar and curls.

Filling: Beat the cheeses and sugar in large bowl with electric mixer until smooth. Add eggs 1 at a time, beating well between each addition. Stir in rind, chocolate and marmalade.

Chocolate Collar and Curls: Cut a strip of baking paper 7cm x 68cm long. Draw a curved line along edge of paper. Cut along curved line.

HAZELNUT NOUGAT ICE-CREAM TERRINE

We used Callard & Bowser Dessert Nougat in this recipe.

1 cup (150g) unroasted hazelnuts
1½ cups (375ml) milk
300ml cream
4 egg yolks
½ cup (110g) caster sugar
1 tablespoon custard powder
¼ cup (60ml) Frangelico
80g packaged dessert nougat, chopped
⅓ cup (80ml) Nutella

CREAMY HAZELNUT SAUCE
¾ cup (180ml) thickened cream
¼ cup (60ml) Nutella

Grease 2 x 8cm x 26cm bar pans, line with plastic wrap, extending wrap 10cm over edges; place pans in freezer.

Spread nuts evenly onto oven tray, toast in moderately hot oven for about 5 minutes or until skins begin to flake. Rub nuts in cloth to remove skins; cool. Cut nuts in half.

Combine milk with cream in medium pan, bring to boil. Meanwhile, whisk egg yolks, sugar and custard powder in medium bowl until combined. Gradually whisk into hot milk mixture; stir over heat, without boiling, until mixture thickens slightly; stir in liqueur, press plastic wrap over surface of custard; cool.

Pour mixture into ice-cream maker, churn according to the manufacturer's instructions. Add nuts and nougat, churn until combined. Add Nutella, churn for further 30 seconds or until Nutella is just marbled through mixture. Spread ice-cream into prepared pans, cover, freeze until firm.

Using an electric or serrated knife, slice ice-cream. Serve with creamy hazelnut sauce.

Creamy Hazelnut Sauce: Combine ingredients in small jug, mix well; cover, refrigerate.

Serves 8.

- Ice-cream can be made 3 days ahead. Sauce can be made a day ahead.
- Storage: Ice-cream, covered, in freezer. Sauce, covered, in refrigerator.
- Freeze: Sauce, not suitable.
- Microwave: Not suitable.

Spring Spring Spring Spring Spring Spring Spring Spring Spring Spring Spring Spring Sp

10

HONEY MOUSSE BEEHIVES

40g butter
5 eggs, separated
3/4 cup (135g) white chocolate Melts
1/4 cup (60ml) honey
2 teaspoons gelatine
2 tablespoons water
300ml thickened cream

TOFFEE BEEHIVES
1½ cups (330g) caster sugar
½ cup (125ml) water

Coat 6 x 1 cup (250ml) dishes with cooking oil spray.

Combine butter, egg yolks, chocolate and honey in medium pan, stir over heat, without boiling, until chocolate is melted. Transfer mixture to large bowl. Meanwhile sprinkle gelatine over water in cup, stand in small pan of simmering water, stir until gelatine is dissolved; stir into chocolate mixture, cover bowl, cool to room temperature.

Fold whipped cream into chocolate mixture. Beat egg whites in medium bowl with electric mixer until soft peaks form, fold into chocolate mixture in 2 batches. Spoon mixture into prepared dishes. Refrigerate 3 hours or overnight. Turn mousses onto plates. Use the empty mousse dishes for shaping the toffee beehives, then place beehives over mousses.

Toffee Beehives: Cover outside of mousse dishes with foil, lightly coat foil with cooking oil spray. Combine sugar and water in medium pan, stir over heat, without boiling, until sugar is dissolved. Boil, uncovered, without stirring, about 10 minutes or until the toffee is golden brown. Stand a few minutes or until the toffee thickens and will just hold its shape when drizzled over foil.

Drizzle toffee around dishes.

When toffee is set, carefully remove from dishes, gently peel away foil.

Serves 6.

■ Mousses best made a day ahead. Toffee beehives can be made about 1 hour before serving.
■ Storage: Mousses, covered, in refrigerator.
■ Freeze: Not suitable.
■ Microwave: Gelatine suitable.

Plate from Waterford Wedgwood

GRAPE GELATO WITH NUTMEG WAFERS

Nutmeg wafers are easy to make; once you get the timing perfect, you'll be able to have 1 oven tray ready to go in the oven, another baking and a third one's baked wafers being shaped.

1.5kg seedless white grapes, approximately
3 egg whites
3/4 cup (165g) caster sugar

NUTMEG WAFERS
1 egg white
1/4 cup (55g) caster sugar
2 tablespoons plain flour
1/2 teaspoon ground nutmeg
30g butter, melted
2 teaspoons cocoa powder

Discard grape stalks; process grapes until smooth. Push mixture through coarse strainer, pressing firmly to extract as much juice as possible. You need 3 1/4 cups (810ml) juice. Pour juice into large shallow cake pan, cover with foil, freeze until just firm.

Beat egg whites in small bowl with electric mixer until soft peaks form. Gradually add sugar, beating until dissolved between additions. Transfer frozen juice to large bowl, quickly beat with electric mixer until just smooth. Add egg white mixture, beat until combined and smooth. Return mixture to pan, cover, freeze until firm. Serve grape gelato with nutmeg wafers.

Nutmeg Wafers: Beat egg white in small bowl with electric mixer until soft peaks form. Gradually add sugar, beating until dissolved between additions. Stir in sifted flour and nutmeg, then cooled butter. Reserve 2 tablespoons of mixture.

Place teaspoons of mixture about 10cm apart on baking paper-lined oven trays, allow 4 per tray, spread with spatula to about 7cm rounds.

Combine reserved mixture with sifted cocoa in small bowl; mix well. Spoon mixture into piping bag fitted with small plain tube. Pipe circles onto wafers to represent grapes. Bake in moderate oven about 5 minutes or until wafers are lightly browned. Lift wafers carefully from trays, place over handle of wooden spoon to give irregularly round shapes; cool on wire racks.

Serves 6 to 8.

- Grape gelato and nutmeg wafers can be made a day ahead.
- Storage: Gelato, covered, in freezer. Wafers, in airtight container.
- Freeze: Wafers not suitable.
- Microwave: Not suitable.

Bowl, jug and large platter from Bondi Storehouse (left); plate from Villeroy & Boch; wire basket from Bondi Storehouse (right)

BAKED PASSIONFRUIT TART

You need about 4 passionfruit for this recipe.

1½ cups (225g) plain flour
⅓ cup (55g) icing sugar mixture
150g cold unsalted butter, chopped
2 egg yolks

FILLING
7 egg yolks
1 cup (220g) caster sugar
1 teaspoon finely grated lemon rind
⅓ cup (80ml) passionfruit pulp
1 cup (250ml) thickened cream

Process flour, sugar and butter until crumbly. Add egg yolks, process until ingredients just come together. Knead dough on floured surface until smooth. Wrap in plastic, refrigerate 30 minutes.

Roll pastry between sheets of baking paper until large enough to line 24cm round loose-based flan tin, ease pastry into tin, trim edge. Cover, refrigerate for 1 hour.

Cover pastry with baking paper, fill with dried beans or rice, place on oven tray. Bake in moderately hot oven for 15 minutes. Remove paper and beans, bake another 10 minutes or until pastry is lightly browned; cool.

Pour filling into pastry case, bake in slow oven about 50 minutes or until just set; cool. Serve at room temperature, dusted with a little sifted icing sugar.
Filling: Combine all ingredients in medium bowl; mix well.

Serves 8.

■ Can be made a day ahead.
■ Storage: Covered, in refrigerator.
■ Freeze: Uncooked pastry suitable.
■ Microwave: Not suitable.

ABOVE: Baked Passionfruit Tart.
LEFT: Grape Gelato with Nutmeg Wafers.

COCONUT AND SOUR CREAM CHEESECAKE

250g packet plain sweet biscuits, finely crushed
125g butter, melted

FILLING
250g packet cream cheese, softened
300ml sour cream
¼ cup (60ml) Malibu
3 eggs
280g can coconut milk
½ cup (45g) coconut, toasted
¼ cup (35g) cornflour
½ cup (110g) caster sugar

TOFFEE BARK
½ cup (110g) sugar

Combine biscuit crumbs with butter in bowl; mix well. Use a flat-bottomed glass to press mixture evenly over base and side of greased 22cm springform tin, refrigerate 30 minutes.

Place tin on oven tray, pour filling into crumb crust. Bake in moderate oven about 1¼ hours or until filling is just firm. Cool cheesecake in oven with door ajar.

Cover cold cheesecake, refrigerate 3 hours or overnight. Serve dusted with sifted icing sugar, if desired, and pieces of toffee bark.

Filling: Beat all ingredients in medium bowl with electric mixer until mixture is creamy.

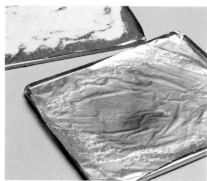

Toffee Bark: Cover an oven tray with foil, lightly coat foil with cooking oil spray. Sprinkle evenly with half the sugar. Place under hot grill for about 2 minutes or until sugar is dissolved and golden brown; cool.

Carefully peel toffee away from foil, break into pieces. Repeat process with remaining sugar.

Serves 8.

■ Cheesecake can be made 3 days ahead. Toffee bark best made on day of serving.
■ Storage: Cheesecake, covered, in refrigerator. Bark in airtight container.
■ Freeze: Not suitable.
■ Microwave: Not suitable.

ITALIAN RICOTTA PINE NUT CAKE

1¼ cups (185g) self-raising flour
1 cup (150g) plain flour
½ cup (60g) packaged
  ground almonds
½ cup (100g) firmly packed
  brown sugar
190g cold butter, chopped
1 egg, lightly beaten
3 teaspoons cold water

FILLING
5 cups (1kg) ricotta cheese
¾ cup (165g) caster sugar
2 egg yolks
1 tablespoon plain flour
½ teaspoon ground cinnamon
¼ cup (60ml) Creme de Cacao
½ cup (80g) pine nuts, toasted
⅓ cup (55g) sultanas, chopped
½ cup (95g) dark chocolate Bits,
  roughly chopped

Lightly grease 24cm springform tin, cover base with foil.

Process all ingredients until just combined. Press dough into a ball, wrap in plastic wrap, refrigerate 30 minutes.

Press three-quarters of the pastry over base and 5cm up side of tin. Wrap remaining pastry in plastic wrap, refrigerate until ready to use.

Spread filling evenly into pastry case; coarsely grate remaining pastry evenly over filling. Bake in moderate oven for about 1¼ hours or until filling is just set. Cool cake in tin, cover cake with foil, refrigerate overnight. Serve with whipped cream, if desired.

Filling: Whisk cheese, sugar, egg yolks, flour, cinnamon and liqueur in large bowl until well combined. Stir in remaining ingredients.

Serves 10 to 12.

■ Best made a day ahead.
■ Storage: Covered, in refrigerator.
■ Freeze: Not suitable.
■ Microwave: Not suitable.

ABOVE: Italian Ricotta Pine Nut Cake.
RIGHT: Warm Mango Galettes.

WARM MANGO GALETTES

1¼ cups (185g) plain flour
1 teaspoon mixed spice
2 tablespoons caster sugar
125g cold butter, chopped
2 teaspoons water, approximately
¼ cup (30g) packaged
    ground almonds
2 tablespoons packaged
    ground hazelnuts
2 tablespoons brown sugar
1 tablespoon plain flour, extra
½ teaspoon ground cinnamon
4 medium (1.75kg) mangoes, sliced
2 tablespoons chopped
    hazelnuts, toasted

CUSTARD SAUCE
1½ cups (375ml) prepared
    pouring custard
⅓ cup (80ml) Malibu

Sift flour, half the mixed spice and caster sugar into medium bowl. Rub in butter, add enough water to mix to a firm dough. Knead dough on floured surface until smooth; wrap in plastic wrap, cover, refrigerate 1 hour.

Roll dough until 3mm thick, cut into 8 x 12cm rounds. Place rounds 5cm apart on greased oven trays. Combine ground nuts, brown sugar, extra flour, cinnamon and remaining mixed spice in small bowl, sprinkle over rounds, leaving 1cm borders; top with mango slices. Bake galettes in moderately hot oven about 25 minutes or until pastry is crisp and browned. Serve warm sprinkled with chopped nuts and dusted with a little sifted icing sugar, if desired. Serve with custard sauce.

Custard Sauce: Whisk custard and liqueur together in jug.

Serves 8.

■ Mango galettes best made just before serving. Custard sauce can be made a day ahead.
■ Storage: Covered, in refrigerator.
■ Freeze: Not suitable.
■ Microwave: Not suitable.

CHOCOLATE CANNOLI

Cannelloni pasta shells make excellent cannoli moulds; they are available in packets of 15 to 16 (instant), or 24 to 26 (regular), but must be discarded after deep-frying. Metal cannoli moulds are available at specialty kitchen shops. If you use metal cannoli moulds, you're ensured of getting a sufficient number of shells to make this recipe.

1½ cups (225g) plain flour
2 tablespoons cocoa powder
2 egg yolks
1 egg
2 tablespoons Creme de Cacao or Tia Maria
1 tablespoon olive oil
1½ tablespoons water, approximately
plain flour, extra
1 egg white
vegetable oil for deep-frying

RICOTTA FILLING
1kg (5 cups) ricotta cheese
½ cup (80g) icing sugar mixture
1⅓ cups (200g) white chocolate Melts, melted
⅓ cup (80ml) Creme de Cacao or Tia Maria

CHOCOLATE SAUCE
⅔ cup (160ml) cream
100g dark chocolate, chopped

Process flour, cocoa, egg yolks, egg, liqueur and olive oil with enough water to form a soft dough, process until the mixture forms a ball. Knead dough on floured surface about 5 minutes or until smooth; wrap in plastic wrap, refrigerate 1 hour.

Divide dough into 2 portions. Roll each portion through pasta machine set on thickest setting. Fold dough in half, roll through machine; dust with a little extra flour, when necessary. Keep rolling dough through machine, adjusting setting so dough becomes thinner with each roll. Roll to second thinnest setting. Cut dough into 24 x 9cm squares, ensure each piece is 5mm short of the ends of the pieces of pasta or metal moulds.

Glass bowl from H.A.G. Imports; stainless steel tray and fork from Ventura Design

Place whichever mould you're using on end of each square.

Roll dough around mould, brush overlapping end with a little egg white, make sure egg white does not touch the mould, press firmly to seal. Repeat with remaining squares.

Deep-fry cannoli in batches in hot vegetable oil until crisp; drain on absorbent paper. Carefully remove warm cannoli shells from moulds; cool. Spoon ricotta filling into large piping bag fitted with plain 1cm tube, pipe the filling into cannoli. Serve chocolate cannoli with chocolate sauce.

Ricotta Filling: Beat cheese and sifted icing sugar in large bowl with electric mixer until smooth, beat in cooled chocolate and liqueur.

Chocolate Sauce: Combine cream and chocolate in small pan, stir over low heat until chocolate is melted.

Serves 8.

- Cannoli shells, ricotta filling and chocolate sauce can all be made a day ahead. Assemble close to serving.
- Storage: Shells in airtight container. Filling and sauce, covered, separately in refrigerator.
- Freeze: Not suitable.
- Microwave: Sauce suitable.

Fabric from St James Furnishings

CREME BRULEE TART

1½ cups (225g) plain flour
2 tablespoons custard powder
125g cold butter, chopped
1 egg yolk
1 tablespoon cold water,
approximately

FILLING
5 egg yolks
⅓ cup (75g) caster sugar
1 vanilla bean
1½ cups (375ml) thickened cream
⅓ cup (80ml) milk

TOPPING
1½ tablespoons brown sugar
1 tablespoon pure icing sugar

Grease 24cm round loose-based flan tin. Process flour, custard powder and butter until just crumbly. Add egg yolk and enough water to make ingredients just cling together. Press dough into a ball, knead gently on floured surface until smooth. Wrap in plastic wrap, refrigerate 30 minutes.

Roll pastry between sheets of baking paper until large enough to line prepared tin. Lift pastry into tin, ease into side, trim edge, refrigerate 30 minutes.

Cover pastry with baking paper, fill with dried beans or rice, place on oven tray. Bake in moderately hot oven for 10 minutes. Remove paper and beans, bake another 10 minutes or until pastry is lightly browned; cool.

Pour filling into pastry case, bake in slow oven about 40 minutes or until the custard is set; cool.

Sift topping evenly over custard, refrigerate 1 hour. Cover pastry edge with foil; place tart under hot grill for about 2 minutes or until sugar is melted and golden brown. If sugar does not melt in 2 minutes, lightly brush topping with water, grill again.

Filling: Whisk egg yolks and sugar in medium bowl until thick and creamy. Split vanilla bean lengthways, scrape seeds into medium pan. Add cream and milk to pan, bring to boil; remove from heat. Whisk hot milk mixture into egg yolk mixture; strain, cool.

Topping: Sift sugars together twice through a fine sieve.

Serves 8.

■ Pastry case can be made a
  week ahead.
■ Storage: In airtight container.
■ Freeze: Uncooked pastry suitable.
■ Microwave: Not suitable.

ABOVE: Creme Brulee Tart.
RIGHT: Rum 'n' Raisin Mascarpone Ice-Cream Sandwich.

RUM 'N' RAISIN MASCARPONE ICE-CREAM SANDWICH

3 egg yolks
½ cup (110g) caster sugar
1 cup (250ml) milk
¼ cup (60ml) dark rum
80g dark chocolate, chopped
¾ cup (180ml) cream
⅓ cup (55g) chopped raisins
1¼ cups (310g) mascarpone cheese
icing sugar mixture

SABLE BISCUITS
1¼ cups (185g) plain flour
¼ cup (40g) icing sugar mixture
100g cold butter, chopped
1 egg yolk

CHOCOLATE SAUCE
⅓ cup (80ml) milk
2 tablespoons cream
1 tablespoon sugar
80g dark chocolate, chopped
20g butter

Whisk egg yolks and sugar in small bowl until pale and thick. Combine milk, rum and chocolate in medium pan, stir over heat, without boiling, until the chocolate is melted. Remove from heat, gradually whisk egg mixture into chocolate mixture, stir over low heat, without boiling, until mixture thickens slightly; press plastic wrap over surface of custard; refrigerate until cold.

Whisk cream, raisins and cheese into chocolate mixture, pour mixture into ice-cream maker, churn following manufacturer's instuctions. Transfer mixture to loaf pan, cover with foil, freeze.

Sandwich sable biscuits with ice-cream, serve with chocolate sauce, dusted with sifted icing sugar.

Sable Biscuits: Process flour, icing sugar and butter until crumbly. Add egg yolk, process until just combined. Knead dough on floured surface, cover with plastic wrap, refrigerate 30 minutes.

Roll dough between sheets of baking paper until about 3mm thick, cut into 12 x 7.5cm rounds, place rounds onto lightly greased oven trays, refrigerate 30 minutes.

Bake rounds in moderately hot oven about 10 minutes or until lightly browned; cool on wire racks.

Chocolate Sauce: Combine milk, cream and sugar in small pan, bring to boil, stirring. Remove from heat, add chocolate and butter, stir until smooth; cool to room temperature.

Serves 6.

- Ice-cream can be made 3 days ahead. Sable biscuits and chocolate sauce can be made a day ahead.
- Storage: Ice-cream, covered, in freezer. Biscuits, in airtight container. Sauce, covered, in refrigerator.
- Freeze: Uncooked pastry suitable.
- Microwave: Sauce suitable.

Plate and jug from Ware Unique

Spring Spring Spring Spring Spring Spring Spring Spring Spring Spring Spring Spring Sp

PINK GRAPEFRUIT ICE-CREAM WITH SPARKLING SORBET

1/2 cup (110g) sugar
1 1/4 cups (310ml) water
1 cup (250ml) pink sparkling wine

GRAPEFRUIT ICE-CREAM
1 3/4 cups (430ml) milk
2 teaspoons grated pink
  grapefruit rind
1/2 cup (125ml) pink grapefruit juice
300ml thickened cream
6 egg yolks
3/4 cup (165g) caster sugar
orange food colouring

Grease 14cm x 21cm loaf pan, line with plastic wrap; place in freezer. Combine sugar and water in small pan, stir over heat, without boiling, until sugar is dissolved. Simmer, uncovered, without stirring, about 5 minutes or until syrup is slightly thickened. Remove from heat, stir in wine, cool 5 minutes. Place mixture in ice-cream maker, churn following manufacturer's instructions.

Working quickly, spoon sorbet onto a large piece of foil, roll into 20cm log, twist ends to secure, freeze 1 hour. Remould sorbet, still in foil, to make an even neater log shape then refreeze until firm.

Spoon half the grapefruit ice-cream into prepared pan. Remove foil from log; press log firmly but gently into centre of ice-cream, top with remaining ice-cream, cover with foil, freeze until firm.
Grapefruit Ice-Cream: Combine milk, rind, juice and cream in medium pan. Whisk egg yolks and sugar in medium bowl until thick and pale; gradually whisk into milk mixture, stir over heat, without boiling, until mixture thickens slightly, strain into large bowl, cover surface with plastic wrap; cool. Tint ice-cream mixture with a tiny drop of colouring, if desired. Place mixture in ice-cream maker, churn following manufacturer's instructions.

Serves 6.

- Can be made a week ahead.
- Storage: Covered, in freezer.
- Microwave: Not suitable.

MILK CHOCOLATE AND HAZELNUT BAVAROIS

We've used Frangelico, a hazelnut-flavoured liqueur.

1 cup (250ml) milk
6 egg yolks
¼ cup (55g) sugar
250g milk chocolate, chopped
½ cup (125ml) Frangelico
2 teaspoons gelatine
1 tablespoon water
300ml thickened cream
1 egg white
drinking chocolate
crushed hazelnuts

Whisk milk, egg yolks and sugar in medium pan, add chocolate, stir over heat, without boiling, until chocolate is melted and mixture thickens slightly. Stir in liqueur. Meanwhile, sprinkle gelatine over water in cup, stand in small pan of simmering water, stir until dissolved; cool 5 minutes. Stir gelatine mixture into custard, press plastic wrap over surface of custard; refrigerate about 1½ hours or until mixture is the consistency of unbeaten egg white.

Fold whipped cream into custard mixture in 2 batches. Beat egg white in small bowl until firm peaks form, gently fold into custard mixture. Divide the mixture among 8 x ⅔ cup (160ml) dishes, refrigerate 3 hours or overnight. Serve sprinkled with sifted drinking chocolate and crushed hazelnuts.

Serves 8.

■ Best made a day ahead.
■ Storage: Covered, in refrigerator.
■ Freeze: Not suitable.
■ Microwave: Gelatine suitable.

Bowl, plate and spoon from Ware Unique

LEMON GELATO WITH SUGARED PASTRY TWISTS

1/3 cup (80ml) water
3/4 cup (165g) caster sugar
1/4 cup (60ml) light corn syrup
1 1/2 cups (375ml) water, extra
1 tablespoon finely grated
    lemon rind
1 1/2 cups (375ml) lemon juice

SUGARED PASTRY TWISTS
1/2 sheet ready-rolled puff pastry
20g butter, melted
2 teaspoons cinnamon sugar
pinch ground cloves

Combine water, sugar and corn syrup in small pan, stir over heat, without boiling, until sugar is dissolved. Simmer, uncovered, without stirring, 4 minutes. Stir in extra water, rind and juice, pour mixture into lamington pan, cover with foil, freeze until just firm.

Working quickly, transfer gelato mixture into large bowl; beat with electric mixer until smooth. Return mixture to pan, cover, freeze until firm. Repeat process once more. Serve lemon gelato with sugared pastry twists.

Sugared Pastry Twists: Using a fluted pastry cutter, cut pastry widthways into 1cm strips. Brush with butter, sprinkle with combined cinnamon sugar and cloves. Twist into decorative shapes, place on lightly greased oven tray. Bake in moderate oven about 8 minutes or until lightly browned; cool on wire rack.

Serves 4 to 6.

- Gelato and sugared pastry twists can be made 3 days ahead.
- Storage: Gelato, covered, in freezer. Pastry twists, in airtight container.
- Freeze: Pastry twists not suitable.
- Microwave: Not suitable.

ABOVE: Lemon Gelato with Sugared Pastry Twists.
LEFT: Milk Chocolate and Hazelnut Bavarois.

CHOCOLATE MOUSSE PUFFS

1 cup (250ml) water
80g butter, chopped
1 cup (150g) plain flour
2 tablespoons cocoa powder
4 eggs
3 medium (540g) oranges
1 cup (250ml) water, extra
1 cup (220g) caster sugar
2/3 cup (100g) dark chocolate
    Melts, melted
drinking chocolate

CHOCOLATE MOUSSE FILLING
125g packet cream cheese,
    softened
2/3 cup (150g) caster sugar
2 egg yolks
1 2/3 cup (250g) white chocolate
    Melts, melted
600ml thickened cream

LIQUEUR SAUCE
3 egg yolks
1/3 cup (75g) caster sugar
1/4 cup (60ml) Grand Marnier
1/2 cup (125ml) cream

Combine water and butter in medium pan, bring to boil, stirring, until butter is melted. Add sifted flour and cocoa all at once, stir vigorously over heat until mixture leaves side of pan and forms a smooth ball.

Transfer mixture to small bowl of electric mixer, beat in eggs 1 at a time, beating until mixture is thick and glossy before adding next egg.

Drop level tablespoons of mixture 4cm apart onto lightly greased oven trays, bake in hot oven about 15 minutes or until pastry is puffed. Using skewer, make a small hole in base of each puff, cool on wire racks. Split puffs in half, use a teaspoon to scoop out any uncooked mixture; return halves, cut side up, to oven trays. Bake in moderately hot oven about 10 minutes or until puffs are crisp; cool on wire racks.

Using a vegetable peeler, peel rind thinly from oranges.

Combine extra water with sugar in medium pan, stir over heat, without boiling, until sugar is dissolved. Add rind, simmer, uncovered, without stirring, about 3 minutes or until mixture is syrupy. Remove rind to a tray covered with baking paper; cool.

Place melted chocolate in small piping bag, pipe 8cm circles onto baking paper, using bag in a continuous motion, overlapping circles. You need 8 completed circles.

Spoon chocolate mousse filling into half of the puffs, replace tops. Serve puffs with liqueur sauce, glace rind, chocolate circles and dusted with sifted drinking chocolate.

Chocolate Mousse Filling: Beat cheese, sugar and egg yolks in large bowl with electric mixer until smooth. Just before melted chocolate sets, beat into cheese mixture then fold in whipped cream in 2 batches. Cover, refrigerate until cold.

Liqueur Sauce: Combine egg yolks, sugar and liqueur in medium bowl, place bowl over pan of simmering water, whisk until mixture is light and creamy; cool. Fold in lightly whipped cream, cover, refrigerate until cold.

Serves 8.

■ Best assembled just before serving. Unfilled puffs, chocolate mousse filling, liqueur sauce and glace rind can be made a day ahead.
■ Storage: Puffs and rind in separate airtight containers. Filling and sauce, covered, separately, in refrigerator.
■ Freeze: Puffs suitable.
■ Microwave: Chocolate suitable.

HONEY BISCUITS WITH CARAMELISED BANANA

60g butter
⅓ cup (65g) firmly packed
  brown sugar
1 tablespoon honey
1 tablespoon hot water
⅓ cup (50g) plain flour

CARAMELISED BANANA
20g butter
2 tablespoons brown sugar
1 medium (200g) banana, sliced

BANANA LIQUEUR CREAM
300ml thickened cream
½ cup (125ml) mascarpone cheese
2 tablespoons icing sugar mixture
¼ cup (60ml) Irish cream liqueur
2 medium (400g) bananas, chopped

Combine butter, sugar and honey in small pan, stir over heat, without boiling, until sugar is dissolved. Simmer, uncovered, without stirring, 2 minutes. Cool for 5 minutes, whisk in water, then flour.

Drop tablespoons of mixture onto baking-paper-lined oven trays; allow 4 biscuits per tray. Bake in moderate oven about 8 minutes or until biscuits are bubbly and browned. Cool biscuits on trays. You need 12 biscuits.

Layer biscuits on plates sandwiched with banana liqueur cream. Dust with a little sifted icing sugar, if desired, then top with caramelised bananas.

Caramelised Banana: Melt butter in small pan, add sugar, stir over heat, without boiling, until sugar is dissolved. Add banana, cook, stirring occasionally, until mixture is caramelised.

Banana Liqueur Cream: Whip cream in medium bowl until firm peaks form; stir in remaining ingredients.

Serves 4.

■ Honey biscuits and banana liqueur cream can be made several hours ahead. Assemble just before serving.
■ Storage: Biscuits in airtight container. Caramelised banana, covered, at room temperature. Banana liqueur cream, covered, in refrigerator.
■ Freeze: Not suitable.
■ Microwave: Caramelised banana suitable.

ABOVE: Honey Biscuits with Caramelised Banana.
RIGHT: Panna Cotta with Fruit Compote.

PANNA COTTA WITH FRUIT COMPOTE

Panna cotta is an Italian favourite and literally means cooked cream.

3 teaspoons gelatine
1¼ cups (310ml) milk
2 cups (500ml) thickened cream
¾ cup (165g) caster sugar
2 teaspoons vanilla essence

FRUIT COMPOTE
1 large (2kg) pineapple, peeled
1½ cups (375ml) Sauternes-style
　　dessert wine
⅓ cup (80ml) water
⅔ cup (150g) caster sugar
1 vanilla bean
12 (120g) prunes
12 (180g) dried peaches
1 medium (70g) lime

Grease 6 x ¾ cup (180ml) dishes. Sprinkle gelatine over ¼ cup (60ml) of the milk, stir to combine, then stand for 5 minutes. Combine remaining milk and cream with sugar in medium pan, stir over heat, without boiling, until sugar is dissolved and milk mixture hot. Remove from heat, stir in gelatine mixture and essence; strain into jug. Pour milk mixture into prepared dishes, cool, cover, refrigerate 3 hours or overnight.

Just before serving, turn panna cotta onto individual plates; serve with fruit compote.

Fruit Compote: Cut pineapple into 8 wedges lengthways, cut core from wedges. Chop 2 wedges roughly, process until finely chopped. Strain and reserve ⅔ cup (160ml) juice; discard pulp. Cut remaining pineapple into 1cm slices. Combine wine, water, sugar and reserved juice in medium pan, stir over heat, without boiling, until sugar is dissolved. Simmer, uncovered, without stirring, about 15 minutes or until liquid becomes thick and syrupy. Split vanilla bean open, add to sugar syrup with the remaining pineapple, prunes and dried peaches. Simmer, uncovered, for 15 minutes, stirring occasionally. Transfer compote to bowl; cool, cover, refrigerate. Using zester, peel shreds of rind from lime, add to compote when cold.

Serves 6.

■ Best made a day ahead.
■ Storage: Covered, separately, in refrigerator.
■ Freeze: Not suitable.
■ Microwave: Not suitable.

Alessi plate from Ventura Design

PASSIONFRUIT PINEAPPLE SORBET WITH MINT SAUCE

You need about 12 passionfruit for this recipe.

1 large (2kg) pineapple, peeled, cored, chopped
½ cup (110g) caster sugar
1 cup (250ml) water
½ cup (125ml) passionfruit pulp
3 egg whites

MINT SAUCE
½ cup (125ml) passionfruit pulp
⅔ cup (160ml) water
2 tablespoons caster sugar
⅓ cup firmly packed fresh mint leaves
½ teaspoon arrowroot
1 teaspoon water, extra

Blend or process pineapple until smooth, push through a strainer; discard pulp. You need 2½ cups (625ml) juice. Combine sugar and water in medium pan, stir over heat, without boiling, until sugar is dissolved. Simmer, uncovered, without stirring, about 10 minutes, or until syrup is thick; cool.

Stir pineapple juice and passionfruit pulp into sugar syrup, pour into 20cm x 30cm lamington pan, cover with foil, freeze until just set and, working quickly, process sorbet with egg whites until smooth, pour into 14cm x 21cm loaf pan, cover, freeze overnight. Serve with mint sauce.

Mint Sauce: Push passionfruit pulp through coarse strainer, reserve juice and 1 teaspoon of the seeds. Combine reserved juice, water, sugar and mint in pan, stir over heat, without boiling, until sugar is dissolved. Stir in blended arrowroot and extra water, simmer gently, stirring about 1 minute or until sauce is slightly thickened; strain. Stir in reserved seeds, cool.

Serves 4 to 6.

- Sorbet can be made up to 3 days ahead. Mint sauce best made just before serving.
- Storage: Sorbet, covered, in freezer.
- Freeze: Sauce not suitable.
- Microwave: Not suitable.

ABOVE: Passionfruit Pineapple Sorbet with Mint Sauce.
RIGHT: Pineapple Coconut Dessert Cake.

PINEAPPLE COCONUT DESSERT CAKE

1 large (2kg) pineapple, peeled, cored
125g butter
½ cup (110g) caster sugar
4 eggs
1 cup (150g) self-raising flour
½ cup (75g) plain flour
½ cup (45g) coconut
¼ cup (40g) semolina

PINEAPPLE ORANGE SYRUP
1 large (300g) orange
1 cup (220g) caster sugar

Grease 21cm baba pan. Process pineapple in batches until roughly chopped, place in medium pan, boil, uncovered, 1 minute; cool.

Drain pineapple into bowl; reserve 1½ cups pulp for cake and ¾ cup (180ml) juice for syrup.

Beat butter and sugar in small bowl with electric mixer until light and fluffy; beat in eggs 1 at a time. Mixture will curdle but will reconstitute later. Transfer to large bowl then add, in 2 batches, the sifted flours, coconut, semolina, and reserved pineapple pulp. Spread mixture into prepared pan, bake in moderate oven for about 55 minutes. Stand cake 5 minutes before turning onto wire rack over tray, pour ⅔ cup (160ml) hot syrup over cake, reserving remaining syrup. Just before serving, top cake with glace rind, drizzle with reserved cold pineapple orange syrup.

Pineapple Orange Syrup: Using a zester, peel shreds of rind from orange. Reserve ¼ cup (60ml) orange juice, discard pulp. Combine sugar with orange rind and juice, and reserved pineapple juice in medium pan, stir over heat, without boiling, until sugar is dissolved. Simmer, uncovered, without stirring, 5 minutes. Strain; reserve glace rind and syrup separately.

Serves 10.

- Best made a day ahead.
- Storage: Cake, in airtight container. Glace rind and reserved syrup, covered, separately in refrigerator.
- Freeze: Cake without syrup suitable.
- Microwave: Not suitable.

Summer

A mousse of fresh raspberries, a frozen parfait made with apricots and macadamias, and ice-creams galore — rockmelon and plum and a trio of berries — who wouldn't look forward with mouthwatering anticipation to the end of a meal in summer? Making the most of the abundance of fruits helps disguise the fact that these recipes are perfectly wicked indulgences!

SUMMER PUDDINGS

300g raspberries
150g blueberries
200g redcurrants
1/3 cup (75g) caster sugar
1/4 cup (60ml) water
1 large (about 11cm x 28cm)
brioche loaf
4 slices white bread

Combine berries, sugar and water in medium pan, stir gently over heat, without boiling, until sugar is dissolved. Simmer, uncovered, without stirring, for about 5 minutes or until juices are released from fruit; strain, reserve liquid.

Lightly grease 4 x 3/4 cup (180ml) dishes, sprinkle with a little extra caster sugar; shake away excess.

Cut brioche into 1cm slices, remove crusts. Place 2 slices together to form a square then, using a 7.5cm cutter, cut through both pieces to make 2 semi-circles that fit base of prepared dishes.

Cut strips of remaining brioche slices to fit sides of dishes. Cut bread slices into 4 x 6.5cm rounds to fit top of dishes.

Lightly dip 1 side of brioche semi-circles and strips in reserved liquid; do not saturate. Line dishes with brioche, dipped side down. Divide fruit mixture and 1/4 cup (60ml) of the reserved liquid among dishes, top with rounds, cover with plastic wrap; weight each pudding with a small can, refrigerate overnight. Turn puddings onto plates, serve with remaining reserved liquid, fresh berries and cream, if desired.

Serves 4.

■ Puddings must be made
   a day ahead.
■ Storage: Covered, in refrigerator.
■ Freeze: Not suitable.
■ Microwave: Not suitable.

GINGERED APRICOT AND CUSTARD PUFFS

2 sheets frozen puff pastry, thawed
1 egg, separated
4 medium (50g) apricots,
thinly sliced

CUSTARD CREAM
½ cup (110g) caster sugar
¼ cup (35g) plain flour
2 cups (500ml) milk
1 teaspoon vanilla essence
6 egg yolks
1 teaspoon chopped glace ginger
½ cup (75g) chopped dried apricots
3 butternut cookies, chopped
½ cup (125ml) thickened cream

SPICED SYRUP
5 cloves
1 stick cinnamon
1 cup (250ml) water
⅓ cup (75g) caster sugar

Custard Cream: Blend sugar and flour with a little of the milk in medium pan, gradually stir in remaining milk. Stir over heat until mixture boils and thickens, simmer 1 minute. Remove from heat, stir in essence and egg yolks. Reserve 1 cup of custard for spiced syrup. Transfer remaining custard to medium bowl, stir in ginger, apricots and cookies; press plastic wrap over surface of the custard; cool. Fold in whipped cream.

Spiced Syrup: Combine cloves, cinnamon, water and sugar in pan, cook, stirring, until sugar is dissolved. Bring to boil, simmer 6 minutes or until syrup thickens slightly, discard cloves and cinnamon stick; cool. Combine syrup with reserved custard.

Serves 4.

- Pastry, custard cream and spiced syrup may be made 3 hours before serving.
- Storage: Custard cream and spiced syrup, covered, separately, in refrigerator. Pastry in airtight container.
- Freeze: Not suitable.
- Microwave: Syrup suitable.

Cut out 4 x 9.5cm apricot shapes from each sheet of pastry, brush shapes lightly with egg white, place on greased oven tray, 4cm apart. Cover each brushed piece with an unbrushed piece of pastry.

Use a sharp knife to lightly mark the surface of the pastry, brush with egg yolk, bake in hot oven, about 12 minutes or until browned and crisp. Split each pastry into 2, re-separating base from lid, return to oven tray for a few minutes to dry out, cool on wire rack. Fill bases with custard cream, top with sliced apricots, then pastry lid, dust with sifted icing sugar, if desired; serve with spiced syrup.

Dessert plate from The Pacific East India Company

CHOCOLATE HONEYCOMB ICE-CREAM TOWERS

We used Violet Crumble chocolate honeycomb bars in this recipe.

2 cups (500ml) milk
300ml cream
5 egg yolks
½ cup (110g) caster sugar
1 tablespoon custard powder
100g dark cooking chocolate,
 finely chopped
¼ cup (60ml) Kahlua or
 Creme de Cacao
50g chocolate honeycomb bars,
 coarsely chopped
1⅓ cups (200g) dark chocolate
 Melts, melted

Grease 6 x ¾ cup (180ml) dishes, line with plastic wrap, bringing wrap 5cm over sides. Freeze until ready to use.

Combine milk and cream in medium pan, bring to boil. Meanwhile, whisk egg yolks, sugar and custard powder in medium bowl, gradually whisk in hot milk mixture. Add dark cooking chocolate, stir until melted, stir in liqueur; cover surface with plastic wrap, cool.

Pour the mixture into ice-cream machine, churn, following manufacturer's instructions. Reserve 1 tablespoon of the chopped chocolate honeycomb; add remaining chocolate honeycomb to machine, churn 1 minute. Spoon mixture into prepared dishes, smooth tops, tap gently on bench to remove air bubbles. Enclose dishes in plastic wrap; freeze until firm.

Finely chop reserved chocolate honeycomb. Spread melted chocolate evenly over 2 sheets of baking paper, each about 26cm x 28cm, sprinkle reserved honeycomb evenly over chocolate, leave to set.

Carefully remove chocolate from paper, break into long wedges, about 3cm x 13cm each.

Turn ice-cream onto plates, remove wrap, gently press chocolate wedges around sides. Serve immediately.

Serves 6.

■ Best made a day ahead.
■ Storage: Ice-cream, covered, in freezer. Chocolate wedges covered, in airtight container.
■ Freeze: Chocolate wedges unsuitable.
■ Microwave: Chocolate suitable.

PLUM ICE-CREAM WITH PECAN BISCOTTI

6 medium (720g) blood plums
2 cups (500ml) milk
1 cup (250ml) cream
1 vanilla bean
6 egg yolks
½ cup (110g) caster sugar
2 tablespoons custard powder
300ml cream, extra

PECAN BISCOTTI
1 cup (150g) plain flour
¼ teaspoon baking powder
½ teaspoon ground cinnamon
½ cup (110g) caster sugar
1 egg, lightly beaten
½ teaspoon vanilla essence
1 teaspoon water
1 cup (100g) pecans, toasted, chopped

Cut a small cross on base of plums, place into large pan of boiling water, return to boil; drain. Place plums in large bowl of cold water, stand 5 minutes; drain. Peel away skins, chop plums coarsely.

Heat milk, cream and split vanilla bean in medium pan; remove bean. Whisk egg yolks, sugar and custard powder together in small bowl, whisk into milk mixture. Whisk over heat, without boiling, until mixture thickens; cover surface of custard with plastic wrap; cool.

Stir plums and extra cream into custard, pour into ice-cream machine, churn following manufacturer's instructions. Serve ice-cream with pecan biscotti.

Pecan Biscotti: Sift flour, baking powder, cinnamon and sugar into medium bowl, stir in egg, essence and water. Turn dough onto floured surface, knead in nuts. Shape dough into 30cm log, place on greased oven tray, bake in moderate oven about 35 minutes or until just brown and crusty; cool on tray.

Using a serrated knife, cut log diagonally into 5mm slices, place in single layer on oven trays, bake in moderate oven about 15 minutes or until biscotti are crisp; cool on wire racks.

Serves 6.

■ Ice-cream can be made 3 days ahead. Biscotti can be made 2 weeks ahead.
■ Storage: Ice-cream, covered, in freezer. Biscotti in airtight container.
■ Microwave: Not suitable.

LEFT: Chocolate Honeycomb Ice-Cream Towers
RIGHT: Plum Ice-Cream with Pecan Biscotti.

Table setting from B.J. Homewares

PASSIONFRUIT CREME BRULEE

You will need about 6 passionfruit for this recipe.

1 egg
5 egg yolks
¼ cup (55g) caster sugar
600ml thickened cream
½ cup (125ml) passionfruit pulp
1½ tablespoons brown sugar
1 tablespoon pure icing sugar

Whisk egg, egg yolks and caster sugar in medium bowl until pale and slightly thickened. Heat cream, without boiling, in medium pan, gradually whisk into egg mixture, strain custard into a jug; stir in passionfruit.

Place 6 x ¾ cup (180ml) ovenproof dishes in baking dish, pour custard into dishes. Pour enough boiling water into baking dish to come halfway up sides of dishes. Bake in moderate oven for about 25 minutes or until set. Remove dishes from water; cool.

Sift brown and icing sugars together twice through a fine sieve, then sift mixture evenly over custards, refrigerate 1 hour. Place custards under hot grill for about 2 minutes or until sugar is melted and golden brown. If sugar does not melt in 2 minutes, lightly brush tops with water, grill again. Refrigerate 3 hours before serving.

Serves 6.

- Can be prepared a day ahead.
- Storage: Covered, in refrigerator.
- Freeze: Not suitable.
- Microwave: Not suitable.

BELOW: Passionfruit Creme Brulee.
RIGHT: Frozen Apricot Amaretto Parfait.

Plates from Villeroy & Boch

SummerSummerSummerSummerSummerSummerSummerSummerSummerSummerSumm

38

Plates from Villeroy & Boch

FROZEN APRICOT AMARETTO PARFAIT

⅓ cup (80ml) water
1 cup (220g) caster sugar
8 egg yolks
1 cup (250ml) thickened cream
¾ cup (180g) mascarpone cheese
¼ cup (60ml) amaretto
100g chopped chocolate
   honeycomb pieces
½ cup (80g) chopped almond
   kernels, toasted
5 large (400g) apricots,
   seeded, sliced

TOFFEE CURLS
¼ cup (55g) caster sugar

Grease 14cm x 21cm loaf pan, cover base and sides with plastic wrap, extending enough wrap over sides so top of pan is completely covered.

Combine water and sugar in small pan, stir over heat, without boiling, until sugar is dissolved. Simmer, without stirring, about 5 minutes or until mixture is slightly thickened. Beat egg yolks in small bowl with electric mixer until thick and creamy. With the motor operating, gradually pour hot syrup in a thin stream onto egg yolks, continue beating about 10 minutes or until mixture has cooled.

Transfer egg mixture to large bowl. Beat cream in small bowl until soft peaks form, stir in cheese and liqueur, then fold in remaining ingredients. Fold into egg mixture, pour into prepared pan, cover with plastic wrap, freeze for 6 hours or overnight, until firm. Turn parfait onto board, remove plastic wrap, cut into 8 slices, then halve each on the diagonal. Stand parfait 5 minutes before serving with toffee curls.

Toffee Curls: Cover back of oven tray with foil, lightly grease foil, sprinkle half the sugar randomly over foil, place under hot grill until sugar is melted and light brown.

Stand toffee about 30 seconds; while it is still warm, peel it away from the foil in strips, curling and shaping the toffee as you remove it. Cool. Repeat process, re-greasing foil, using remaining sugar.

Serves 8.

▪ Parfait best made a day ahead. Toffee curls best made close to serving.
▪ Storage: Parfait, covered, in freezer.
▪ Microwave: Not suitable.

Plate from Villeroy & Boch

ROCKMELON CHEESECAKES WITH SPONGE BISCUITS

Any Sauternes-style dessert wine can be used instead of the orange muscat.

1 medium (1.6kg) rockmelon, halved, seeded
½ medium (800g) honeydew melon, seeded
¼ small (2kg) watermelon, seeded
½ cup (75g) finely chopped macadamias, toasted
125g shortbread biscuits
30g butter, melted

FILLING
250g packet cream cheese, softened
1 cup (250g) mascarpone cheese
⅔ cup (150g) caster sugar
1 tablespoon lemon juice
¼ cup (60ml) orange muscat dessert wine
5 teaspoons gelatine
2 tablespoons water
½ cup (125ml) thickened cream

SPONGE BISCUITS
1 egg
¼ cup (55g) caster sugar
⅓ cup (50g) plain flour

Coat 6 x ¾ cup (180ml) moulds lightly with cooking oil spray, cover bases with baking paper; place moulds on tray. Using a 2cm melon baller, scoop 1 rockmelon half into balls; scrape out and reserve flesh of other half. Repeat both steps with honeydew and watermelon.

Blend or process reserved rockmelon flesh until just smooth; you will need ¾ cup (180ml) rockmelon puree for the filling; reserve remaining puree for serving. Blend or process reserved honeydew and watermelon flesh, separately, until smooth.

Blend or process nuts and biscuits together until finely chopped, transfer mixture to small bowl, stir in butter. Divide mixture among moulds, press down firmly over bases. Refrigerate 15 minutes or until firm. Spoon filling into moulds, refrigerate for 3 hours or overnight.

Turn cheesecakes onto serving plates, top with melon balls, spoon some of each melon puree around cheesecakes, serve with sponge biscuits.

Filling: Beat cheeses and sugar in medium bowl with electric mixer until smooth. Add juice, wine and reserved ¾ cup (180ml) rockmelon puree, beat until combined. Push mixture through fine strainer into large bowl. Combine the gelatine and water in small cup, stand in a pan of simmering water, stir until dissolved. Stir gelatine mixture into cheese mixture, mix well. Fold in the whipped cream.

Sponge Biscuits: Beat egg and sugar in small bowl with electric mixer until pale in colour, fold in sifted flour. Spoon mixture into piping bag fitted with 5mm tube. Pipe 12cm lines about 4cm apart on greased baking-paper-lined oven trays. Bake in moderately hot oven about 6 minutes or until lightly browned; cool on trays.

Serves 6.

▪ Cheesecakes can be made a day ahead. Sponge biscuits can be made a week ahead.
▪ Storage: Cheesecakes, covered, in refrigerator. Biscuits, in airtight container.
▪ Freeze: Not suitable.
▪ Microwave: Gelatine suitable.

CHERRY ALMOND TART

1 cup (150g) plain flour
¼ cup (35g) rice flour
2 tablespoons caster sugar
90g cold butter, chopped
1 egg, lightly beaten
2 teaspoons cold water,
   approximately
500g cherries, seeded

FILLING
70g butter
⅓ cup (75g) caster sugar
1 egg
⅔ cup (80g) packaged
   ground almonds
1 tablespoon plain flour

GLAZE
2 tablespoons apricot jam
1 tablespoon water

Grease 11cm x 35cm rectangular or 20cm round loose-based flan tin. Sift flours and sugar into medium bowl, rub in butter. Add egg and enough water to make ingredients cling together. Knead dough on floured surface until smooth, cover with plastic wrap, refrigerate 30 minutes.

Roll pastry between sheets of baking paper until large enough to line prepared tin. Lift pastry into tin, ease into sides, trim edges, lightly prick base with fork; refrigerate 30 minutes.

Cover pastry with baking paper, fill with dried beans or rice. Place tin on oven tray, bake in moderately hot oven 10 minutes, remove paper and beans, bake another 10 minutes or until pastry is lightly browned; cool.

Spread filling into pastry case, top with cherries, press gently into almond mixture, bake in moderate oven about 40 minutes; cool. Brush tart evenly with hot glaze.

Filling: Beat butter, sugar and egg in small bowl with electric mixer until light and fluffy. Add almonds, beat until thick; stir in flour.

Glaze: Combine jam and water in small pan, stir over heat until mixture comes to the boil; push through strainer.

Serves 6.
- Can be made a day ahead.
- Storage: Airtight container.
- Freeze: Uncooked pastry suitable.
- Microwave: Glaze suitable.

LEFT: Cherry Almond Tart.
RIGHT: Passionfruit Liqueur Souffles.

Vases from House; plates from Villeroy & Boch

Setting from Villeroy & Boch

PASSIONFRUIT LIQUEUR SOUFFLES

You will need about 4 passionfruit for this recipe.

2 egg yolks
1/3 cup (80ml) passionfruit pulp
2 tablespoons La Grande Passion liqueur or Grand Marnier
1/2 cup (80g) icing sugar mixture
4 egg whites

Grease 4 x 3/4 cup (180ml) ovenproof dishes. Sprinkle base and sides evenly with a little caster sugar; shake away excess. Place dishes on oven tray.

Whisk egg yolks, passionfruit, liqueur and 2 tablespoons of the icing sugar in medium bowl until combined. Beat egg whites in small bowl with electric mixer until soft peaks form; add remaining icing sugar, continue beating until firm peaks form. Fold about a quarter of the egg white mixture into passionfruit mixture, then fold in remaining egg white mixture. Spoon into prepared dishes, bake in moderately hot oven about 12 minutes or until souffles are puffed. Serve immediately dusted with a little sifted icing sugar.

Serves 4.

■ Souffles must be made just before serving.
■ Freeze: Not suitable.
■ Microwave: Not suitable.

VERY-BERRY ICE-CREAM

150g blackberries, halved
150g raspberries
250g strawberries, chopped
³/₄ cup (165g) caster sugar
2 cups (500ml) milk
8 egg yolks
2 tablespoons caster sugar, extra
300ml cream

BLACKBERRY COULIS
400g blackberries
2 tablespoons icing sugar mixture

CHOCOLATE SHAPES
1 cup (150g) dark chocolate
   Melts, melted

Grease 3 x 8cm x 26cm bar cake pans, cover bases with baking paper to extend 2cm above sides of pans.

Combine berries and sugar in medium pan, stir over heat, without boiling, until sugar is dissolved. Simmer, stirring occasionally, for about 15 minutes or until mixture thickens and is reduced to about 1½ cups (375ml). Cool, then refrigerate until cold.

Bring milk to boil in medium pan. Whisk egg yolks and extra sugar in medium bowl until creamy, gradually whisk into hot milk. Stir over heat, without boiling, until mixture thickens slightly. Transfer to large bowl. Press plastic wrap over surface of custard; cool. Refrigerate until cold.

Stir berry mixture and cream into custard, divide evenly among prepared pans. Cover with foil, freeze until just firm. Beat ice-cream in large bowl with electric mixer until just smooth. Return ice-cream to pans, cover with foil; freeze until firm.

Serve ice-cream with blackberry coulis, chocolate shapes and, if desired, whole berries and mint leaves.

Blackberry Coulis: Blend or process berries and sugar until smooth; strain.
Chocolate Shapes: Spread chocolate evenly onto baking paper-lined oven tray; allow to just set.

Cut chocolate into 5cm-square decorative shapes. When completely set, lift off gently with spatula. Cut shapes in half diagonally.

Serves 6 to 8.

- Ice-cream can be made up to 3 days ahead; blackberry coulis the day before; chocolate shapes best made on day of serving.
- Storage: Ice-cream, covered, in freezer. Coulis, covered, in refrigerator. Chocolate in cool, dry place.
- Freeze: Coulis suitable.
- Microwave: Chocolate suitable.

FROZEN ROCKMELON MACADAMIA PARFAIT

You need to seed, peel and chop a quarter of a medium rockmelon for this recipe. We tinted the rockmelon a pale apricot colour using a combination of yellow and red food colourings.

3/4 cup (180ml) rockmelon puree
1 cup (220g) caster sugar
60g butter, melted
3 egg yolks
1½ tablespoons lemon juice
1½ cups (375ml) thickened cream
3/4 cup (110g) macadamias,
    halved, toasted

RASPBERRY SAUCE
200g raspberries
2 tablespoons honey
1 tablespoon Grand Marnier
1 tablespoon lime juice

Wash and dry a 1-litre cardboard milk or juice carton. Staple opening at top to secure. Place carton on its side, cut a rectangular opening in topmost side, leaving 1 short end attached, to serve as a flap. Push melon puree through a fine strainer; reserve.

Combine sugar, butter, egg yolks and juice in small bowl over pan of simmering water; beat with electric mixer for 15 minutes or until slightly thickened. Remove from heat, continue to beat for 5 minutes or until mixture is thick and cool. Transfer mixture to large bowl, fold in whipped cream in 2 batches; reserve 1 cup of cream mixture.

Fold melon puree into remaining mixture; tint, if desired. Place carton on tray with flap uppermost, fill with half the melon mixture; freeze until firm. Combine reserved cream mixture with nuts, spoon over melon layer; freeze until firm. Pour remaining melon mixture into carton, close flap; freeze overnight.

To serve, cut carton to remove parfait. Cut parfait into 12 slices, cut slices in half diagonally. Stack triangles on plates. Serve with raspberry sauce.

Raspberry Sauce: Push berries through fine strainer into small bowl, stir in remaining ingredients.

Serves 6.

- Recipe can be made 3 days ahead.
- Storage: Parfait, covered in freezer. Raspberry sauce, covered, in refrigerator.
- Freeze: Sauce suitable.
- Microwave: Not suitable.

Plate from Bondi Storehouse; bottle and tassle from Sirocco Homewares

CHOCOLATE NUT PATE WITH FRUIT IN LIME SYRUP

1/4 cup (35g) raw cashews
1/4 cup (35g) pistachio nuts
1/4 cup (35g) unroasted hazelnuts
30g butter
1/2 cup (125ml) sweetened
    condensed milk
2 cups (300g) dark chocolate Melts
2 tablespoons Tia Maria or Kahlua

FRUIT IN LIME SYRUP
3/4 cup (165g) sugar
1 1/2 cups (375ml) water
1 tablespoon lime juice
1 vanilla bean
2 medium (230g) carambolas, sliced
4 medium (120g) figs, quartered
150g raspberries
170g boysenberries

CHOCOLATE WAVES
3/4 cup (100g) dark chocolate
    Melts, melted

Toast nuts on oven tray in moderate
oven for about 10 minutes. Grease 8cm
x 26cm bar cake pan, cover base and
sides with baking paper. Combine butter, milk and chocolate in medium pan,
stir over heat, without boiling, until mixture is smooth; stir in nuts and liqueur.
Spread mixture into prepared pan,
cover with foil, refrigerate overnight.

Remove pate from pan, cut into
slices. Layer slices in single layer on
tray between sheets of baking paper;
cover, refrigerate until ready to serve.
Serve pate with fruit in lime syrup and
chocolate waves.

Fruit in Lime Syrup: Combine sugar
and water in medium pan, stir over
heat, without boiling, until sugar is
dissolved. Add juice and split bean,
simmer, uncovered, without stirring,
about 10 minutes or until mixture has
thickened slightly; cool. Combine fruit
in bowl, add syrup, cover and refrigerate.

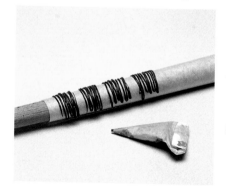

Chocolate Waves: Secure a sheet of
baking paper around a small rolling pin
or piece of dowling. Using a paper piping bag, pipe chocolate back and forth
over paper, forming chocolate waves.
Allow to set before peeling off paper.

Glass compote from H.A.G. Imports; plate from Waterford Wedgwood; fabric from St James Furnishings

Serves 8.
- Pate can be made up to 3 weeks
  ahead. Fruit in lime syrup and
  chocolate waves best made
  on day of serving.
- Storage: Pate, in airtight container,
  in refrigerator.
- Freeze: Not suitable.
- Microwave: Chocolate suitable.

*LEFT: Frozen Rockmelon
Macadamia Parfait.
ABOVE: Chocolate Nut Pate
with Fruit in Lime Syrup.*

REDCURRANT AND HAZELNUT TART

1½ cups (225g) plain flour
2 tablespoons icing sugar mixture
2 tablespoons packaged
    ground hazelnuts
125g cold butter, chopped
1 egg yolk
1 tablespoon water, approximately
400g redcurrants

FILLING
1½ cups (225g) roasted hazelnuts
4 eggs
½ cup (100g) firmly packed
    brown sugar
½ cup (125ml) honey
½ cup (125ml) light corn syrup
1 teaspoon vanilla essence
2 teaspoons grated orange rind
50g butter, melted

TOPPING
2 teaspoons gelatine
1 tablespoon water
300g jar redcurrant jelly

Grease 21cm x 28.5cm rectangular or 23cm round loose-based flan tin.

Sift flour and sugar into medium bowl, stir in nuts, rub in butter. Add egg yolk and enough water to make the ingredients cling together. Knead dough on floured surface until smooth, wrap in plastic wrap, refrigerate 30 minutes.

Roll pastry between sheets of baking paper until large enough to line prepared tin. Lift pastry into tin, ease into sides, trim edges. Lightly prick base with fork, refrigerate 30 minutes.

Cover pastry with baking paper, fill with dried beans or rice, place on oven tray. Bake in moderately hot oven 15 minutes. Remove paper and beans carefully from pastry case, bake another 15 minutes or until lightly browned; cool.

Pour filling into pastry case, bake in moderate oven about 45 minutes or until set; cool. Place redcurrants over filling, brush with topping, refrigerate until topping is set.

Filling: Rub hazelnuts with cloth to remove skins; chop nuts in half. Whisk eggs, sugar, honey, corn syrup, essence and rind together in medium bowl; stir in butter and nuts.

Topping: Sprinkle gelatine over water in cup, stand in pan of simmering water, stir until dissolved. Warm jelly in small bowl over pan of simmering water, stir in gelatine mixture.

Serves 6 to 8.

■ Pastry case can be made 3 days ahead. Assemble tart on day of serving.
■ Storage: Pastry case, in airtight container.
■ Freeze: Uncooked pastry suitable.
■ Microwave: Topping suitable.

BLACK FOREST SOUFFLES WITH KIRSCH CREAM

400g cherries, seeded, halved
1/3 cup (75g) caster sugar
2 tablespoons Kirsch
1 tablespoon lemon juice

CHOCOLATE SOUFFLE TOPPING
50g butter
1 tablespoon cocoa powder
1/2 cup (125ml) buttermilk
2 tablespoons caster sugar
125g dark chocolate, chopped
2 egg yolks
4 egg whites
2 tablespoons caster sugar, extra

KIRSCH CREAM
1 cup (250ml) thickened cream
1 tablespoon caster sugar
1/2 teaspoon ground nutmeg
1½ tablespoons Kirsch

Combine cherries, sugar, liqueur and juice in small pan, stir over heat, without boiling, until sugar is dissolved. Simmer, uncovered, without stirring, about 10 minutes or until mixture is thick and syrupy; cool.

Lightly grease 6 x 3/4 cup (180ml) souffle dishes, sprinkle base and sides with sugar; shake away excess sugar. Place dishes on oven tray, divide cherry mixture among prepared dishes, then top with chocolate souffle topping mixture, bake in hot oven about 12 minutes, or until lightly puffed. Serve immediately with Kirsch cream.

Chocolate Souffle Topping: Melt butter in small pan, add cocoa, stir until smooth. Stir in buttermilk, heat without boiling; remove from heat. Add sugar and chocolate, stir until smooth; transfer to large bowl; stir in egg yolks. Beat egg whites in small bowl with electric mixer until soft peaks form, add extra sugar, beat until dissolved. Fold into chocolate mixture in 2 batches.

Kirsch Cream: Beat cream, sugar and nutmeg in small bowl until soft peaks form, stir in liqueur.

Serves 6.

■ Cherry syrup and Kirsch cream can be made a day ahead. Chocolate souffle mixture can be prepared 3 hours ahead. Fold egg white mixture into chocolate souffle mixture just before cooking.
■ Storage: Covered, separately, in refrigerator.
■ Freeze: Not suitable.
■ Microwave: Not suitable.

LEFT: Black Forest Souffles with Kirsch Cream.
RIGHT: Passionfruit Ice-Cream with Coconut Crisps.

Plates from Villeroy & Boch; cutlery from Victoria Spring Designs

PASSIONFRUIT ICE-CREAM WITH COCONUT CRISPS

You will need about 8 passionfruit for this recipe; coconut wafers are easy to make; once you get the timing perfect, you'll be able to have 1 tray ready to go in the oven, another baking and a third tray's baked wafers being shaped.

2 cups (500ml) milk
8 egg yolks
2/3 cup (150g) caster sugar
2/3 cup (160ml) passionfruit pulp
300ml thickened cream

COCONUT CRISPS
40g unsalted butter
1/4 cup (55g) caster sugar
2 tablespoons plain flour
1 1/2 tablespoons milk
1/3 cup (30g) coconut

Bring milk to boil in medium pan. Whisk egg yolks and sugar in medium bowl until creamy, gradually whisk into hot milk, stir over heat, without boiling, until mixture thickens slightly; press plastic wrap over surface of custard; cool, then refrigerate 1 hour or until cold.

Stir passionfruit into custard, then add cream, pour into ice-cream maker, churn following manufacturer's instructions. Serve passionfruit ice-cream with coconut crisps.

Coconut Crisps: Grease oven trays, cover with baking paper. Beat butter and sugar in small bowl with electric mixer until light and fluffy. Stir in sifted flour and milk, then coconut, stir until just combined. Drop teaspoons of mixture onto prepared trays about 10cm apart, allow 4 per tray, spread with a spatula into 3cm rounds. Bake in moderately hot oven about 6 minutes or until crisps are lightly browned around edges. Stand 30 seconds, then slide a metal spatula under each crisp.

Quickly shape crisps over the greased handle of a metal utensil; leave until firm. Transfer crisps to wire rack. Makes about 25.

Serves 6.

■ Passionfruit ice-cream best made a day ahead. Coconut crisps best made on day of serving.
■ Storage: Ice-cream, covered, in freezer. Coconut crisps, in airtight container.
■ Freeze: Crisps not suitable.
■ Microwave: Not suitable.

SUMMER BERRY CLAFOUTI

While we used the best of the season here, any combination of berries would be delicious.

200g boysenberries
200g blackberries
150g raspberries
100g blueberries
3 eggs
1/3 cup (75g) caster sugar
1 teaspoon vanilla essence
1/3 cup (50g) plain flour
1 tablespoon self-raising flour
3/4 cup (180ml) milk

Grease 4 x 1¾ cup (430ml) shallow ovenproof dishes; place on oven tray. Divide berries among dishes. Whisk eggs, sugar and essence in medium bowl until frothy, whisk in sifted flours and milk, whisk until just combined. Pour mixture, over the back of a dessertspoon, into dishes. Bake in moderate oven about 35 minutes or until clafouti are set. Serve warm, dusted with sifted icing sugar and rich cream, if desired.

Serves 4.

- ■ Best made just before serving.
- ■ Freeze: Not suitable.
- ■ Microwave: Not suitable.

BELOW: Summer Berry Clafouti.
RIGHT: Nectarine Ice-Cream Cakes.

NECTARINE ICE-CREAM CAKES

**7 medium (875g) nectarines,
    peeled, chopped
300ml thickened cream
½ cup (125ml) milk
5 egg yolks
½ cup (110g) caster sugar
2 tablespoons Grand Marnier
¼ cup (40g) icing sugar mixture**

BISCUITS
**80g butter
½ teaspoon vanilla essence
¼ cup (50g) firmly packed
    brown sugar
1 egg yolk
1 cup (150g) plain flour**

TOFFEE
**¾ cup (165g) sugar
¾ cup (180ml) water**

Blend or process half the chopped nectarines until smooth. Combine cream and milk in small pan, bring to boil, remove from heat. Beat egg yolks and caster sugar in small bowl with electric mixer until thick and creamy; beat in nectarine puree then, gradually, the hot cream mixture; cool. Pour mixture into a deep 19cm square cake pan, cover with foil; freeze 3 hours or until firm.

Beat ice-cream in large bowl with electric mixer until smooth and creamy; return mixture to pan; cover, freeze until firm. Blend or process remaining nectarines with liqueur and icing sugar until smooth. Sandwich biscuits with ice-cream; serve with nectarine puree, toffee and, if desired, extra wedges of nectarines.

Biscuits: Beat butter, essence, sugar and egg yolk in small bowl with electric mixer until just combined; stir in sifted flour. Knead dough on lightly floured surface until smooth; cover, refrigerate 30 minutes.

Roll dough between sheets of baking paper until about 4mm thick, place on tray, refrigerate 30 minutes. Cut out 12 x 7.5cm rounds, place rounds about 3cm apart on greased oven trays. Bake in moderate oven about 8 minutes or until just firm. Cool biscuits on wire rack.

Toffee: Combine sugar and water in small pan, stir over heat, without boiling, until sugar is dissolved. Simmer, uncovered, without stirring, about 10 minutes or until a dark caramel colour.

Drizzle hot toffee into decorative shapes onto 2 foil-covered oven trays. When set, peel foil away carefully.

Serves 6.

■ Ice-cream and biscuits can be
  made 2 days ahead. Toffee best
  made close to serving.
■ Storage: Ice-cream, covered,
  in freezer. Biscuits, in airtight
  container.
■ Microwave: Not suitable.

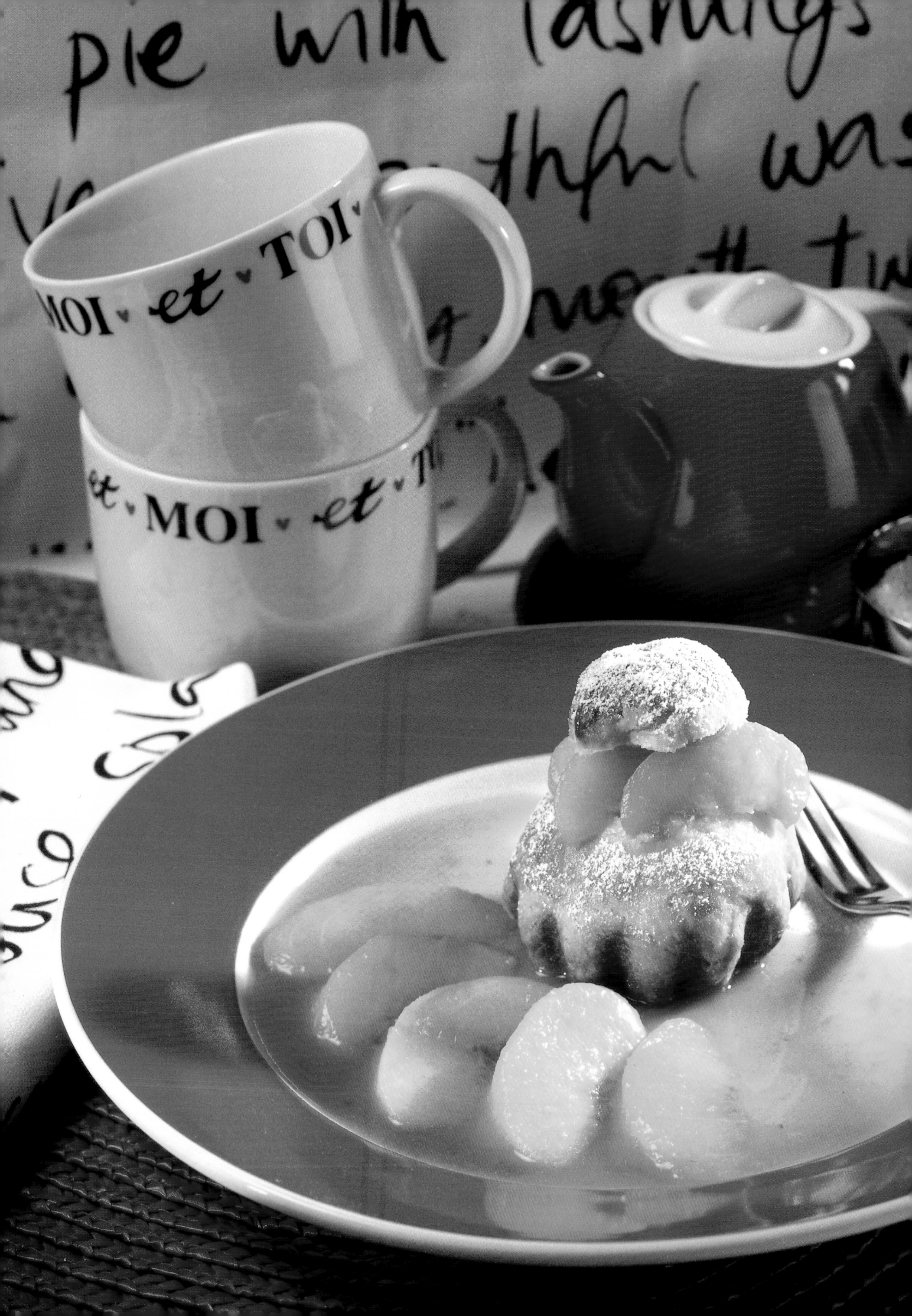
MOI et TOI
et MOI et
pie with
was

BRIOCHE WITH CARAMELISED PEACHES

2 teaspoons dried yeast
2 tablespoons warm water
2 tablespoons caster sugar
2 cups (300g) plain flour
½ teaspoon salt
2 eggs
125g butter
2 medium (65g) glace peaches,
    finely sliced
1 egg yolk
2 tablespoons milk

CARAMELISED PEACHES
8 medium (1.6kg) firm
    slipstone peaches
40g butter
½ cup (100g) firmly packed
    brown sugar
¼ cup (60ml) water
1 tablespoon Grand Marnier

Grease 8 x ½ cup (125ml) fluted oven-proof moulds, place on oven tray. Combine yeast, water and 2 teaspoons of the sugar in small bowl; cover, stand in warm place about 10 minutes, or until mixture is frothy.

Sift remaining sugar, flour and salt into medium bowl, stir in yeast mixture and eggs. Turn dough onto floured surface, knead about 10 minutes, or until dough comes together.

Divide butter into 8 portions; on a cool surface, knead each portion into dough, kneading well after each addition. Dough should be smooth and glossy. Place dough in large bowl, cover, stand in warm place about 1 hour or until doubled in size.

Knead glace peaches into dough, divide dough into 8 portions. Remove one-eighth of the dough from each portion. Roll both the smaller and larger portions into rounds. Place larger rounds in prepared moulds, flatten slightly; brush with combined egg yolk and milk, top with small rounds of dough. Push a thick wooden butcher's skewer through both pieces of dough from top to base of mould to secure brioche; remove skewer. Brush brioche with egg mixture, stand in warm place about 15 minutes or until risen.

Bake brioche in moderately hot oven 10 minutes, reduce heat to moderate, bake about another 8 minutes or until brioche sound hollow when tapped with finger. Turn immediately onto wire rack. Serve dusted with a little sifted icing sugar and caramelised peaches.

Caramelised Peaches: Seed, peel and thickly slice peaches. Heat butter in large pan, add peaches, cook over medium heat, stirring occasionally, about 5 minutes, or until peaches begin to soften; remove from pan. Add sugar, water and liqueur to same pan, stir over heat, without boiling, until the sugar is dissolved. Return the peaches to pan, simmer, uncovered, about 5 minutes or until mixture is slightly thickened.

Serves 8.

■ Brioche dough can be made a day ahead, placed in moulds. Caramelised peaches best made just before serving.
■ Storage: Unbaked brioche, in refrigerator, before glazing with egg mixture and last rising.
■ Freeze: Baked brioche suitable.
■ Microwave: Not suitable.

BAKLAVA WITH LYCHEES AND TOFFEE CUSTARD

3 cups (750ml) water
1½ cups (330g) caster sugar
¼ cup (60ml) honey
1 vanilla bean
2 teaspoons grated fresh ginger
1kg lychees, peeled

BAKLAVA
1½ cups (235g) pine nuts, toasted
1½ cups (225g) shelled pistachio
   nuts, toasted
1 teaspoon ground cinnamon
2 teaspoons grated orange rind
9 sheets fillo pastry
100g butter, melted

TOFFEE CUSTARD
1 cup (250ml) milk
2 cups (500ml) thickened cream
1 vanilla bean
½ cup (110g) caster sugar
6 egg yolks
1 egg
2 tablespoons pure icing sugar

Combine water, sugar, honey and split vanilla bean in medium pan, stir over heat, without boiling, until the sugar is dissolved. Simmer, uncovered, without stirring, 5 minutes; stir in ginger.

Reserve 2 cups (500ml) sugar syrup for baklava. Add lychees to remaining syrup; cool. Cover lychee mixture, refrigerate 3 hours. Discard vanilla bean.

Serve baklava on plates with lychees, syrup and toffee custard.

Baklava: Grease a deep 23cm square cake pan. Process nuts, cinnamon and rind until finely chopped. Cut the pastry sheets in half widthways. Using the cake pan as a guide, cut pastry same size as base. Layer 3 pastry halves together, brushing each layer with butter, place in prepared pan. Sprinkle with one-fifth of the nut filling. Repeat layering with remaining pastry, butter and filling, finishing with pastry.

Using a sharp knife, cut top layer of pastry into quarters, then cut each quarter in half diagonally. Bake baklava in moderately hot oven for 30 minutes, reduce heat to slow, bake for another 10 minutes. Pour the reserved sugar syrup over baklava; cool in pan.

Toffee Custard: Combine milk, cream and split vanilla bean in medium pan, bring slowly up to the boil; remove from heat, stand 10 minutes; discard vanilla bean. Whisk sugar, egg yolks and egg into cream mixture, pour into a 2 litre/ 8 cup flameproof shallow dish, place in baking dish with enough boiling water to come halfway up sides of flameproof dish. Bake in moderate oven about 40 minutes or until custard is just set. Remove from water; cool. Refrigerate the custard overnight. Sift icing sugar over custard, grill under hot grill until top is slightly caramelised.

Serves 8.

- Lychees and baklava can be made 3 days ahead. Toffee custard best prepared a day ahead.
- Storage: Lychees and toffee custard, covered, separately, in refrigerator. Baklava, in airtight container.
- Freeze: Not suitable.
- Microwave: Not suitable.

PEACHES WITH SABAYON AND CINNAMON SNAPS

1 litre (4 cups) water
2 cups (440g) caster sugar
½ cup (125ml) orange juice
¼ cup (60ml) Grand Marnier
1 cinnamon stick
2 cloves
½ teaspoon ground cardamom
6 medium (1kg) peaches
¾ cup (180g) mascarpone cheese

CINNAMON SNAPS
30g butter
2 tablespoons caster sugar
2 tablespoons plain flour
½ teaspoon ground cinnamon

SABAYON
4 egg yolks
1 tablespoon caster sugar

Combine water, sugar, juice, liqueur and spices in large pan, stir over heat, without boiling, until sugar is dissolved. Simmer, uncovered, for 3 minutes. Add peaches, simmer, uncovered, for about 15 minutes or until tender. Remove from heat, cool. Peel peaches; transfer, with syrup, to large bowl, cover, refrigerate for 3 hours or overnight.

Serve peaches with mascarpone, cinnamon snaps and sabayon.

Cinnamon Snaps: Combine butter, sugar and 2 tablespoons of the syrup in medium pan, stir over heat without boiling, until sugar is dissolved; simmer, uncovered, without stirring, 2 minutes.

Remove from heat, stir in flour and cinnamon, then cook 1 minute or until mixture begins to catch on base of pan. Cool until mixture can be handled, roll level teaspoons of mixture into balls, then roll into 10cm sticks.

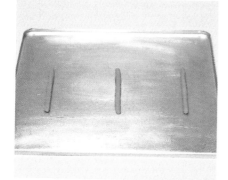

Place 3 sticks 10cm apart on greased oven tray. Bake in moderate oven about 5 minutes or until lightly browned. Remove from oven, stand for 1 minute before lifting, with metal spatula, onto wire rack to cool. Repeat with the remaining mixture.

Coffee plunger, cup and saucer from Caffe Bianchi

Sabayon: Combine egg yolks, sugar and ½ cup (125ml) of the syrup in top of double saucepan or bowl, place over simmering water; whisk constantly (or beat with rotary beater or electric mixer) about 8 minutes or until mixture thickens slightly and becomes frothy. Do not allow water in bottom saucepan to touch base of top pan. Serve immediately.

Serves 6.

- Peach mixture can be made 2 days ahead. Cinnamon snaps best made close to serving. Sabayon must be made just before serving.
- Storage: Peaches, covered, in refrigerator.
- Freeze: Not suitable.
- Microwave: Not suitable.

OPPOSITE: Baklava with Lychees and Toffee Custard.
ABOVE: Peaches with Sabayon and Cinnamon Snaps.

FRESH RASPBERRY MOUSSES

Frozen raspberries can be substituted for fresh, but they should be thawed before using.

500g raspberries
2 egg yolks
1/3 cup (75g) caster sugar
2 teaspoons gelatine
2 tablespoons water
1 cup (250ml) thickened cream
2 tablespoons raspberry jam

JELLY
2/3 cup (160ml) Sauternes-style
**   dessert wine**
2 tablespoons caster sugar
2 teaspoons gelatine
2 tablespoons water

Push half the berries through a sieve, discard seeds; reserve 1 tablespoon of puree for jelly.

Beat egg yolks and sugar in small bowl with electric mixer until pale and thick, fold in puree. Sprinkle gelatine over water in cup, stand in small pan of simmering water, stir until dissolved, cool 5 minutes; stir into berry mixture. Fold whipped cream into berry mixture, pour into 4 x 1 cup (250ml) dessert glasses, refrigerate 3 hours or until set.

Top mousses with remaining berries, then jelly mixture; refrigerate until set. Brush berries with warmed jam just before serving. Serve mousses with rich cream, if desired.

Jelly: Combine the wine, sugar and reserved puree in small pan, stir over heat, without boiling, until the sugar is dissolved. Simmer, uncovered, without stirring, for 1 minute. Sprinkle gelatine over water in cup, stand in small pan of simmering water, stir until dissolved. Stir gelatine into wine mixture; cool in refrigerator until the consistency of unbeaten egg white before using.

Serves 4.

- Best made a day ahead.
- Storage: Covered, in refrigerator.
- Freeze: Not suitable.
- Microwave: Gelatine suitable.

Dessert glass and napkin ring from Home & Garden on the Mall; resin plate and cream cup by Dinosaur Designs; metal plate from Lady Chef; fabric from St James Furnishings

LEFT: Fresh Raspberry Mousses.
RIGHT: Cherry Ricotta Cheesecake.

CHERRY RICOTTA CHEESECAKE

2 cups (300g) plain flour
1/3 cup (75g) caster sugar
125g cold butter, chopped
1 egg, lightly beaten
2 teaspoons iced water,
   approximately
1/3 cup (50g) dark chocolate Melts

FILLING
2 1/2 cups (500g) ricotta cheese,
   sieved
3/4 cup (180g) mascarpone cheese
1/2 cup (110g) caster sugar
1 tablespoon grated orange rind
1 teaspoon ground ginger
3 eggs
2 tablespoons plain flour

POACHED CHERRIES
500g cherries, seeded
1 cup (220g) caster sugar
1 cup (250ml) water
2 tablespoons Grand Marnier
1 tablespoon lemon juice

ORANGE AND CHERRY SAUCE
1/3 cup (80ml) orange juice
1 tablespoon Grand Marnier

Grease a deep 22cm round cake pan. Sift flour and sugar into medium bowl, rub in butter. Add egg and enough water to make ingredients cling together. Knead dough on floured surface until smooth, cover with plastic wrap, refrigerate 30 minutes.

Roll pastry between sheets of baking paper to a 25cm round. Press pastry over base of prepared pan, use back of spoon to press pastry 6cm up side of pan; refrigerate 30 minutes.

Trim pastry with sharp knife to make an even edge that comes about 5cm up the side of pan, place pan on oven tray. Spread one-third of the filling into pastry case, sprinkle evenly with chocolate Melts, then another third of the filling. Top with poached cherries, then the remaining filling. Bake in moderate oven about 1 hour or until filling is firm. Serve ricotta cheesecake dusted with a little sifted icing sugar and orange and cherry sauce.

Filling: Beat cheeses, sugar, rind and ginger in small bowl with electric mixer until smooth. Beat in eggs 1 at a time, beating well between additions. Stir in sifted flour.

Poached Cherries: Combine all ingredients in medium pan, stir over heat, without boiling, until sugar is dissolved. Simmer, uncovered, without stirring, about 15 minutes or until the mixture is slightly thickened. Drain the cherries, reserve syrup.

Orange and Cherry Sauce: Combine reserved syrup, strained orange juice and liqueur in small jug.

Serves 10 to 12.

■ Can be made up to 2 days ahead.
■ Storage: Covered, separately, in refrigerator.
■ Freeze: Not suitable.
■ Microwave: Poached cherries suitable.

Autumn

The wide range of wonderful fruits and nuts that appear at the end of summer more than makes up for the disappearance of peaches and berries for another year. They seem intended for a starring role in desserts that look spectacular, taste delicious and hint at the other sumptuous treats still to come during the colder months.

FRESH FIG AND MASCARPONE TARTLETS

1 cup (150g) plain flour
1 tablespoon custard powder
1 tablespoon caster sugar
100g cold unsalted butter, chopped
1 egg yolk
1 teaspoon grated orange rind
2 teaspoons water, approximately
2 large (160g) fresh figs

TOFFEE
1¼ cups (275g) caster sugar
½ cup (125ml) water
¼ cup (40g) blanched almonds, toasted
½ cup (125ml) strained orange juice
2 tablespoons water

MASCARPONE CREAM
½ cup (125ml) thickened cream
200g mascarpone cheese

Grease 4 x 10cm round loose-based deep flan tins. Sift flour, custard powder and sugar into medium bowl, rub in butter, stir in egg yolk, rind and enough water to mix to a soft dough. Knead dough on floured surface until smooth, wrap in plastic, refrigerate 1 hour.

Roll pastry between sheets of baking paper until large enough to line prepared tins. Lift pastry into tins, press into sides, trim edges, place tins on oven tray, prick bases with fork. Cover pastry with baking paper, fill with dried beans or rice, bake in moderate oven 10 minutes. Remove paper and beans, bake another 10 minutes or until lightly browned; cool.

Halve figs, cut each half into 3 wedges, ready for dipping in toffee.

Place pastry cases on serving plates, fill with mascarpone cream, top each with toffee-coated fig wedges and toffee strands; pour warm orange syrup around tartlets.

Toffee: Cover 3 oven trays with foil. Combine sugar and water in small pan, stir over heat, without boiling, until sugar is dissolved. Simmer, uncovered, without stirring, until mixture turns golden brown; remove from heat.

Dip fig wedges into toffee, place on 1 oven tray to set. Place nuts on another oven tray, pour over half the remaining toffee, stand until set. Break almond toffee into pieces, then blend or process until finely crushed.

Gently reheat remaining toffee; working quickly, dip fork into pan and drizzle long thin strands of toffee onto remaining oven tray.

Add orange juice and water to any toffee left in pan, simmer about 5 minutes or until mixture is syrupy.

Mascarpone Cream: Whip cream in small bowl until firm peaks form, fold in mascarpone in 2 batches, then finely crushed almond toffee.

Serves 4.

- Pastry cases can be made 3 days ahead. Recipe best assembled just before serving.
- Storage: Pastry cases, in airtight container.
- Freeze: Uncooked pastry suitable.
- Microwave: Not suitable.

POACHED PLUMS WITH PASTRY LEAVES

8 medium (1kg) blood plums
2 cups (500ml) water
½ cup (110g) caster sugar
1 cinnamon stick
3 cardamom pods, bruised
10cm strip orange rind
3 cloves
2cm piece fresh ginger, peeled

PASTRY LEAVES
½ cup (75g) plain flour
1 tablespoon caster sugar
30g cold butter, chopped
1 egg yolk
1 tablespoon cold water,
    approximately
1 egg, lightly beaten
1 tablespoon caster sugar, extra

Cut a small cross in base of each plum, place plums into pan of boiling water; drain immediately. Transfer to bowl of cold water; drain, peel away skins.

Combine water with remaining ingredients in pan, stir over heat, without boiling, until sugar is dissolved. Simmer, uncovered, without stirring, about 10 minutes or until reduced to about 1½ cups (375ml). Strain syrup into bowl; cool. Add plums to syrup, cover, refrigerate 3 hours or overnight. Serve plums with syrup and pastry leaves.

Pastry Leaves: Process flour, sugar and butter until crumbly. Add egg yolk and enough water to make ingredients cling together. Knead dough on floured surface until smooth; cover, refrigerate 30 minutes.

Roll pastry between sheets of baking paper until 3mm thick, cut 12 leaf shapes from pastry; place on greased oven trays. Using a blunt knife, mark veins on leaves, brush with egg, sprinkle with extra sugar. Bake in moderately hot oven about 10 minutes or until golden brown; cool on trays.

Serves 4.

■ Best made a day ahead.
▨ Storage: Plums in syrup, covered, in refrigerator. Pastry leaves, in airtight container.
▨ Freeze: Not suitable.
▨ Microwave: Plums suitable.

BELOW: Poached Plums with Pastry Leaves.
RIGHT: Warm Fruit Salad in Pomegranate Syrup.

WARM FRUIT SALAD IN POMEGRANATE SYRUP

6 large (1.8kg) oranges, peeled
2 medium (320g) pomegranates
1 litre (4 cups) water
1½ cups (330g) caster sugar
2 tablespoons orange flower water
250g strawberries, halved

WHIPPED MASCARPONE
2 egg yolks
2 tablespoons caster sugar
1 cup (250g) mascarpone cheese
1 tablespoon Galliano

Remove all white pith from oranges, slice thickly. Remove and discard skin and pith from pomegranates. Reserve ¼ cup of the seeds, combine remaining seeds with the water in large pan. Bring to boil, strain, reserve liquid, discard seeds. Return liquid to pan, add sugar, stir, without boiling, until dissolved. Add oranges, simmer, uncovered, 30 minutes. Remove oranges from pan, simmer syrup 30 minutes or until reduced to about 2 cups (500ml). Stir in orange flower water; add fruit; cool. Stir in reserved seeds. Serve warm fruit with syrup and whipped mascarpone.

Whipped Mascarpone: Beat egg yolks and sugar in small bowl with electric mixer until thick and pale. Stir in mascarpone and liqueur.

Serves 6.

- Fruit mixture can be made a day ahead.
- Storage: Covered, in refrigerator.
- Freeze: Not suitable.
- Microwave: Not suitable.

CREAMY LIME AND NASHI FLAN

1 tablespoon macadamia nut oil
3/4 cup (105g) macadamia nuts
1 cup (150g) plain flour
100g cold butter, chopped
1/4 cup (55g) caster sugar
1 egg yolk

FILLING
250g quark cheese
3 egg yolks
1/2 cup (110g) caster sugar
1/4 cup (60ml) cream
1 teaspoon grated lime rind
1 tablespoon lime juice

NASHI TOPPING
1 litre (4 cups) water
1 cup (220g) sugar
1/2 cup (125ml) lemon juice
4 medium (900g) nashis,
 halved, cored

GLAZE
2/3 cup (160ml) lime marmalade
1 teaspoon finely shredded
 lime rind

Lightly grease 21cm x 29cm rectangular or 23cm round loose-based flan tin.

Heat oil in small pan, add nuts, stir over low heat about 10 minutes or until nuts are browned; cool. Process nut mixture until nuts are coarsely chopped.

Sift flour into medium bowl, rub in butter. Add nuts, sugar and egg yolk; stir until just combined. Knead dough on floured surface until smooth. Using floured fingers or back of spoon, press dough over base and sides of prepared tin; cover, refrigerate 30 minutes.

Cover pastry with baking paper, fill with dried beans or rice, place on oven tray. Bake in moderately hot oven 10 minutes. Remove paper and beans, bake in moderate oven another 10 minutes or until lightly browned; cool.

Pour filling into flan case, bake in moderately slow oven about 25 minutes or until almost set in centre; cool, then refrigerate until firm.

Just before serving, top flan with sliced nashi, brush with glaze.

Filling: Beat all ingredients in small bowl with electric mixer until smooth.

Nashi Topping: Combine water, sugar and juice in medium pan, stir over heat, without boiling, until sugar is dissolved. Meanwhile, cut nashi into 5mm slices, add to sugar syrup, simmer, uncovered, about 15 minutes or until nashi are tender. Drain, discard syrup, pat nashi dry with absorbent paper.

Glaze: Melt marmalade gently in small pan; stir in rind.

Serves 6 to 8.

■ Flan case and filling can be made a day ahead.
■ Storage: Flan case in airtight container. Filling, covered, in refrigerator.
■ Freeze: Not suitable.
■ Microwave: Glaze suitable.

ABOVE: Creamy Lime and Nashi Flan.
RIGHT: Cinnamon Figs with Walnut Stars.

CINNAMON FIGS WITH WALNUT STARS

**100g cold unsalted butter,
   finely chopped**
¼ cup (40g) icing sugar mixture
1 egg yolk
2 tablespoons ground walnuts
¾ cup (105g) plain flour
**2 tablespoons chopped
   walnuts, toasted**

DRAMBUIE CREAM
300ml thickened cream
300ml sour cream
½ cup (80g) icing sugar mixture
2 teaspoons Drambuie
3 (60g) dried figs, finely chopped

CINNAMON FIGS
6 large (480g) fresh figs
2 tablespoons caster sugar
¼ teaspoon ground cinnamon

CHOCOLATE STICKS
**⅓ cup (50g) white chocolate
   Melts, melted**
**⅓ cup (50g) dark chocolate
   Melts, melted**

Using a wooden spoon, stir butter and sugar together in medium bowl until just combined, stir in egg yolk then ground walnuts and sifted flour. Press ingredients together, knead gently on floured surface until smooth; cover, refrigerate 1 hour.

Divide dough in half, roll each half between sheets of baking paper until 3mm thick. Cut out 18 x 8.5cm star shapes, place about 3cm apart on greased oven trays. Bake in moderate oven about 12 minutes or until lightly browned. Cool stars on trays, dust with extra sifted icing sugar, if desired. Sandwich 3 stars with drambuie cream. Serve with chopped walnuts, cinnamon figs and chocolate sticks.

Drambuie Cream: Beat creams, sugar and liqueur in small bowl, with electric mixer until thick, stir in figs.

Cinnamon Figs: Halve figs lengthways, sprinkle with combined sugar and cinnamon; grill until caramelised.

Chocolate Sticks: Fill 2 separate piping bags, 1 with white chocolate, the other with dark chocolate.

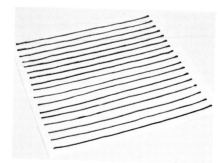

Pipe separate long, thin lines of each chocolate onto baking paper. When set, break into different length sticks.

Serves 6.

- Drambuie cream and figs best made just before serving. Stars and chocolate sticks can be made up to 2 days ahead.
- Storage: Covered, separately, in airtight containers.
- Freeze: Not suitable.
- Microwave: Chocolate suitable.

ORANGE AND FIG CHEESECAKE

½ cup (85g) Brazil nuts
1 cup (125g) plain sweet
    biscuit crumbs
80g butter, melted
1 cup (250ml) orange juice
250g dried figs, finely chopped
1 cinnamon stick
pinch ground cloves

FILLING
250g packet cream cheese,
    softened
1 tablespoon grated orange rind
¾ cup caster sugar
1 teaspoon vanilla essence
1 cup (250g) mascarpone cheese
2 eggs, separated

Grease 22cm springform tin. Blend or process nuts until fine, combine in small bowl with crumbs and butter; mix well. Press mixture over base of prepared tin, refrigerate until firm.

Combine juice, figs, cinnamon and cloves in small pan, simmer, uncovered, about 10 minutes, or until figs have absorbed almost all the liquid; cool. Discard cinnamon stick, spread fig mixture evenly into tin, place on oven tray.

Pour filling over fig mixture, bake in moderately slow oven about 1¼ hours or until cheesecake is just firm in centre. Turn oven off, cool cheesecake in oven with door ajar. Refrigerate cheesecake at least 3 hours or overnight. Serve topped with mint leaves, shredded orange rind and sifted icing sugar, if desired.

Filling: Beat cream cheese, rind and sugar in medium bowl with electric mixer until combined. Add essence, cheese and egg yolks, beat until combined. In a small bowl, beat egg whites until soft peaks form, fold into cheese mixture.

■ Can be made 2 days ahead.
■ Storage: Covered, in refrigerator.
■ Freeze: Not suitable.
■ Microwave: Not suitable.

Setting from Morris Home & Garden Wares

QUINCE SPONGE PUDDING

4 medium (1.25kg) quinces
3 cups (750ml) water
1½ cups (330g) caster sugar
4 cloves
1 cinnamon stick
2 star anise
2 tablespoons icing sugar mixture
¼ teaspoon ground cinnamon

SPONGE TOPPING
3 eggs
½ cup (110g) caster sugar
¼ cup (35g) plain flour
¼ cup (35g) self-raising flour
¼ cup (35g) cornflour

Peel, core and slice quinces, place in 2.5 litre/10-cup shallow ovenproof dish. Combine water, sugar, cloves, cinnamon and star anise in medium pan, stir over heat, without boiling, until sugar is dissolved. Simmer, uncovered, without stirring, 2 minutes. Pour syrup over quinces, cover, bake in moderately hot oven about 2 hours or until quinces are tender and pink.

Carefully drain away 2 cups (500ml) of hot liquid from quinces. Spread hot quinces with sponge topping. Bake in moderate oven about 30 minutes or until browned. Dust with sifted icing sugar and cinnamon, serve with cream and ice-cream, if desired.

Sponge Topping: Beat eggs in small bowl with electric mixer until thick and creamy. Gradually add sugar, beating until dissolved between each addition. Fold in sifted flours.

Serves 6 to 8.

■ Best made just before serving. Quince mixture can be made a day ahead.
■ Storage: Quince mixture, covered, in refrigerator.
■ Freeze: Not suitable.
■ Microwave: Not suitable.

NUTTY CARAMEL FLANS

1½ cups (225g) plain flour
2 tablespoons custard powder
100g cold butter, chopped
1 egg yolk
2 tablespoons iced water,
    approximately

NUTTY CARAMEL FILLING
¼ cup (35g) chopped unroasted
    hazelnuts
¼ cup (25g) chopped pecans
¼ cup (35g) chopped raw peanuts
160g butter
⅓ cup (65g) firmly packed
    brown sugar
¼ cup (60ml) thickened cream

VANILLA SPICE CREAM
300ml thickened cream
½ teaspoon ground cinnamon
¼ teaspoon ground nutmeg
2 tablespoons icing sugar mixture
1 teaspoon vanilla essence

Process flour, custard powder and butter until mixture is crumbly; add egg yolk and enough water to make ingredients just cling together. Knead dough on floured surface until smooth, cover; refrigerate 30 minutes.

Divide pastry into 6 portions. Roll each portion between sheets of baking paper into rounds large enough to line 6 x 9cm round loose-based flan tins. Lift pastry into tins, press into sides, trim edges, place tins on oven tray.

Cover pastry with baking paper, fill with dried beans or rice. Bake in moderately hot oven 10 minutes. Remove paper and beans carefully from pastry cases, bake another 10 minutes or until lightly browned; cool.

Divide filling among pastry cases, bake in moderate oven about 15 minutes or until filling is just set. Serve warm with vanilla spice cream.

Nutty Caramel Filling: Spread nuts onto oven tray, toast in moderate oven about 5 minutes. Combine butter and sugar in small pan, stir over heat, without boiling, until sugar is dissolved. Add nuts and cream, bring to boil, remove from heat.

Vanilla Spice Cream: Beat all ingredients in small bowl until soft peaks form.

Serves 6.

▪ Can be made a day ahead.
▪ Storage: Covered, in refrigerator.
▪ Freeze: Uncooked pastry suitable.
▪ Microwave: Not suitable.

Plates from Waterford Wedgwood; glasses from H.A.G. Imports; fabric from St James Furnishings

LEFT: Quince Sponge Pudding.
RIGHT: Nutty Caramel Flans.

BAKED NASHI WITH PISTACHIO FILLING

60g amaretti biscuits
1/3 cup (85g) roughly chopped
glace apricots
1/4 cup (35g) shelled pistachio
nuts, toasted
30g butter, melted
2 teaspoons roughly chopped
glace ginger
1/4 teaspoon ground allspice
6 medium (1.4kg) nashi
1/3 cup (80ml) apricot jam, warmed
1/4 cup (60ml) Grand Marnier
or Cointreau
2 teaspoons thinly sliced
pistachio nuts
freshly grated nutmeg

ORANGE LIQUEUR CUSTARD
300ml thickened cream
1 cup (250ml) milk
6 egg yolks
2/3 cup (150g) caster sugar
1 tablespoon Grand Marnier
or Cointreau

Process biscuits, apricots, toasted nuts, butter, ginger and allspice until just combined.

Using an apple corer, core nashi, working from the base of each nashi, taking care not to pierce skin at stem end. Score nashi, using a small, sharp knife, from top to base into 8 even sections, keeping the stem end intact. Push biscuit mixture into cavity of nashi. Place nashi, base side down, in greased baking dish, brush with combined strained jam and liqueur. Bake, uncovered, in moderate oven about 1 hour or until tender, basting every 15 minutes. Serve nashi with orange liqueur custard. Sprinkle with sliced nuts and nutmeg.

Orange Liqueur Custard: Bring cream and milk to boil in medium pan. Whisk egg yolks and sugar in medium bowl until creamy; gradually whisk into hot cream mixture. Stir over heat, without boiling, until mixture thickens slightly; stir in liqueur.

Serves 6.

■ Nashi best made just before serving. Orange liqueur custard can be made a day ahead.
■ Storage: Orange liqueur custard, covered, in refrigerator.
■ Freeze: Not suitable.
■ Microwave: Not suitable.

BELOW: Baked Nashi with Pistachio Filling.
RIGHT: Mini Lemon Tortes.

MINI LEMON TORTES

6 eggs
1 cup (220g) caster sugar
1½ cups (225g) self-raising flour
¼ cup (60ml) hot milk
caster sugar, extra

FILLING

1 cup (250ml) lemon butter
2 tablespoons Grand Marnier
   or Cointreau
2 teaspoons grated lemon rind
2 tablespoons lemon juice

CHOCOLATE STARS

1⅔ cups (250g) white chocolate
   Melts, melted

SYRUP

2 cups (440g) caster sugar
1 cup (250ml) water
4 small (400g) lemons
¼ cup (60ml) lemon juice
yellow food colouring

Grease 2 x 26cm x 32cm Swiss roll pans, cover bases and sides with baking paper.

Beat eggs in medium bowl with electric mixer until thick and pale; gradually add sugar, beating until dissolved between each addition. Fold in sifted flour with milk, in 2 batches. Spread mixture between prepared pans. Bake in hot oven about 10 minutes or until lightly browned.

Meanwhile, place 2 sheets of baking paper on bench, sprinkle evenly with extra sugar. When sponges are cooked, turn immediately onto paper; cool 10 minutes. Cut each sponge into 12 x 6.5cm rounds. Spread 1 side of each round with filling, sandwiching 3 rounds together. Decorate each torte with chocolate stars, top with lemon wedges and syrup.

Filling: Combine all ingredients in small pan, stir over heat, without boiling, until lemon butter is melted; cool 10 minutes before using.

Chocolate Stars: Spread chocolate on baking-paper-lined tray into a layer about 2mm thick. When chocolate is almost set, cut into 5.5cm star shapes. When stars are set, peel from paper.

Syrup: Combine sugar and water in medium pan, stir over heat, without boiling, until sugar is dissolved. Boil, uncovered, without stirring, about 8 minutes or until slightly thickened. Add quartered lemons and juice, boil another 4 minutes; tint with colouring, if desired. Remove lemons from syrup with a slotted spoon, drain on wire rack; reserve syrup.

Serves 8.

■ Sponges and chocolate stars can be prepared a day ahead. Assemble tortes just before serving.
■ Storage: Separately, in airtight containers.
■ Freeze: Sponges suitable.
■ Microwave: Chocolate suitable.

HAZELNUT PLUM TART

1 cup (150g) plain flour
1/4 cup (35g) self-raising flour
2 tablespoons custard powder
1/3 cup (55g) icing sugar mixture
3/4 cup (75g) packaged ground
   hazelnuts
125g cold butter, chopped
2 tablespoons iced water,
   approximately

FILLING
6 large (900g) blood plums
2 eggs
1/3 cup (65g) firmly packed
   brown sugar
2 tablespoons plain flour
2 tablespoons buttermilk
1/4 teaspoon ground cardamom

Process flours, custard powder, sugar, nuts and butter until crumbly. Add enough water to make ingredients cling together. Knead dough on floured surface until smooth, cover, refrigerate 30 minutes.

Roll pastry between sheets of baking paper until large enough to line 21cm x 29cm rectangular or 23cm round loose-based flan tin. Lift pastry into tin, press into sides, trim edges, place on oven tray, refrigerate 30 minutes.

Cover pastry with baking paper, fill with dried beans or rice, bake in moderately hot oven 10 minutes, remove beans, bake in moderate oven another 10 minutes until lightly browned; cool.

Place plums cut side down in pastry case, pour in egg mixture. Bake in moderate oven about 40 minutes or until browned. Serve warm or cold with cream or ice-cream, if desired.

Filling: Cut plums in half, remove stones, place plums in pan of boiling water; drain immediately. Transfer to large bowl of cold water, drain, peel away skins; drain plums on absorbent paper. Whisk eggs and sugar in jug, whisk in remaining ingredients.

Serves 6 to 8.

▧ Can be made a day ahead.
▧ Storage: Covered, in refrigerator.
▧ Freeze: Uncooked pastry suitable.
▧ Microwave: Not suitable.

Platter and napkin ring from Sirocco Homewares; bowl from Myer/Grace Bros

PAW PAW AND CITRUS GRANITA

1 medium (180g) orange
1 large (120g) lime
1¼ cups (310ml) water
¾ cup (165g) sugar
1 tablespoon glucose syrup
1 cinnamon stick
2 cloves
1 small (600g) paw paw, chopped
½ cup (125ml) orange juice
⅓ cup (80ml) lime juice

Use a vegetable peeler to remove rind thinly from orange and lime.

Combine rind, water, sugar, glucose, cinnamon and cloves in medium pan, stir over heat without boiling, until sugar is dissolved. Simmer, uncovered, without stirring, 5 minutes; cool. Strain sugar syrup into large bowl.

Blend or process paw paw until smooth, stir into sugar syrup with juices, pour into lamington pan, cover with foil, freeze 30 minutes. Whisk mixture, cover, return to freezer, for 1 hour.

Whisk mixture again, cover with foil, freeze until firm.

Serves 4 to 6.

■ Best made a day ahead.
■ Storage: Covered, in freezer.
■ Microwave: Not suitable.

ABOVE: Paw Paw and Citrus Granita.
LEFT: Hazelnut Plum Tart.

BAKED QUINCES IN ORANGE SYRUP

3 large quinces
1 medium (180g) orange
1¼ cups (275g) caster sugar
1 cup (250ml) water
⅓ cup (80ml) orange juice
½ teaspoon orange flower water

Wipe quinces with damp cloth, prick skins all over with skewer. Wrap quinces individually in foil, stand upright, close together in ovenproof dish. Bake in moderately hot oven about 1 hour or until just tender. Halve quinces, place cut side down in same baking dish.

Meanwhile, use a vegetable peeler to peel wide strips of rind thinly from orange. Combine rind, sugar, water, juice and flower water in small pan. Stir over heat, without boiling, until sugar is dissolved; simmer, uncovered, without stirring, 5 minutes. Remove rind with a slotted spoon to wire rack over tray, reserve syrup.

Pour syrup over quinces. Bake, uncovered, turning occasionally to coat with syrup, in moderately hot oven about 1 hour or until quinces are soft and pink.

Serves 4 to 6.

- ■ Can be made 3 hours ahead.
- ■ Storage: Covered, separately, at room temperature.
- ■ Freeze: Not suitable.
- ■ Microwave: Not suitable.

SPICED FRUIT COMPOTE WITH RICOTTA CREAM

Any Sauternes-style wine can be used instead of the orange muscat.

1½ cups (375ml) orange muscat
½ cup (125ml) water
⅓ cup (80ml) orange juice
¼ cup (60ml) lime juice
¾ cup (165g) sugar
4 small (400g) carambola, sliced
6 (190g) fresh dates, seeded, halved
7 (150g) dried figs, halved
¾ cup (105g) dried apricots
2 cinnamon sticks
1 vanilla bean
5 cardamom pods, bruised
½ teaspoon finely grated lime rind
¼ cup (35g) shelled pistachio
    nuts, chopped

RICOTTA CREAM
1½ cups (300g) ricotta cheese
2 tablespoons icing sugar mixture
½ teaspoon ground cinnamon
¼ cup (60ml) cream

Combine muscat, water, juices and sugar in pan, stir over heat, without boiling, until sugar is dissolved. Simmer, uncovered, without stirring, about 15 minutes or until syrup is slightly thickened. Add carambola, dates, dried fruits, cinnamon, split vanilla bean, cardamom and rind to syrup. Simmer, uncovered, stirring occasionally, about 15 minutes or until fruit is tender. Cool syrup, cover, refrigerate 3 hours or overnight. Discard vanilla bean and cinnamon stick. Serve fruit mixture with ricotta cream and nuts.

Ricotta Cream: Beat cheese, icing sugar and cinnamon in small bowl with electric mixer until smooth. Stir in cream.

Serves 6 to 8.

■ Best made a day ahead.
■ Storage: Covered, separately, in refrigerator.
■ Freeze: Not suitable.
■ Microwave: Not suitable.

ABOVE: Spiced Fruit Compote with Ricotta Cream.
LEFT: Baked Quinces in Orange Syrup.

HONEY LIME BAVAROIS WITH CHOC-COMB

You will need a 13cm-square piece of plastic bubble wrap to make the choc-comb; wash and dry well before use. You will also need about 8 limes for this recipe.

1 cup (250ml) buttermilk
6 egg yolks
3/4 cup (165g) caster sugar
2 tablespoons honey
1 tablespoon finely grated lime rind
1 tablespoon lime juice
3 teaspoons gelatine
1 tablespoon water
1 egg white
300ml thickened cream

SYRUP
1 cup (220g) caster sugar
2/3 cup (160ml) water
1 tablespoon finely grated lime rind
1/2 cup (125ml) apple juice
1/3 cup (80ml) lime juice
1 1/2 tablespoons gin

CHOC-COMB
**1 cup (150g) white chocolate
Melts, melted**

Lightly oil 6 x 1/2 cup (125ml) moulds. Whisk buttermilk, egg yolks, sugar and honey together in medium pan, stir over heat, without boiling, until custard thickens slightly; stir in rind and juice, transfer to large bowl.

Sprinkle gelatine over water in cup, stand in small pan of simmering water, stir until dissolved; cool 5 minutes. Stir gelatine mixture into custard; cover surface with plastic wrap, refrigerate about 1 hour or until mixture is the consistency of unbeaten egg white.

Whisk egg white in small bowl until soft peaks form. Fold whipped cream into custard mixture in 2 batches, then fold in egg white. Spoon mixture into prepared moulds; refrigerate about 3 hours or until set. Turn bavarois onto serving plates, serve with syrup and choc-comb.

Syrup: Combine sugar, water, rind and juices in small pan, stir over heat, without boiling, until sugar is dissolved. Simmer, uncovered, without stirring, about 15 minutes or until mixture thickens; stir in gin.

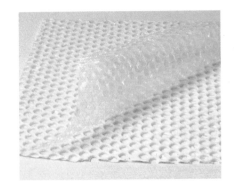

Choc-Comb: Spread chocolate thinly over rounded side of bubble wrap; leave to set at room temperature. Break choc-comb into decorative pieces.

Serves 6.

- Bavarois and choc-comb can be made a day ahead.
- Storage: Covered, separately, in refrigerator.
- Freeze: Not suitable.
- Microwave: Gelatine and chocolate suitable.

Setting from Dinosaur Designs

Plate from Waterford Wedgwood; glass from H.A.G. Imports; spoon from Victoria Spring Designs

TIRAMISU WITH LIQUEUR CUSTARD

3/4 cup (180ml) hot water
1 tablespoon dry instant coffee
1/2 cup (125ml) Kahlua or Tia Maria
14 sponge-finger biscuits
1 teaspoon gelatine
1 tablespoon water
50g dark chocolate, chopped
2 tablespoons milk
1/3 cup (55g) icing sugar mixture
600ml thickened cream
1 1/2 cups (375g) mascarpone cheese
cocoa powder

LIQUEUR CUSTARD
1 1/2 cups (375ml) milk
2 egg yolks
1/4 cup (55g) sugar
1 tablespoon custard powder
1 tablespoon Kahlua or Tia Maria

Grease 2 x 8cm x 26cm bar pans, cover base and sides with plastic wrap, extending wrap 10cm over sides.

Combine water and coffee in medium bowl, stir until dissolved; stir in 1/3 cup (80ml) of the liqueur, cool.

Trim ends from 12 biscuits to fit prepared pans, reserve ends. Dip trimmed biscuits quickly into coffee mixture, place in single layer in prepared pans. Reserve remaining coffee mixture. Coarsely chop remaining biscuits and reserved ends, add to reserved coffee mixture; mix well.

Sprinkle gelatine over water in cup, stand in small pan of simmering water, stir, until gelatine is dissolved.

Combine chocolate and milk in small pan, stir over low heat until chocolate is melted, add hot gelatine mixture; cool.

Beat icing sugar and 2/3 cup (160ml) of the cream in small bowl until soft peaks form, transfer to large bowl. Fold in mascarpone, in 2 batches, then remaining liqueur and chocolate mixture, spread evenly into pans, gently tap pans to remove any air bubbles.

Top with the reserved chopped biscuit mixture, cover, refrigerate for about 3 hours, or until set.

Turn tiramisu onto plastic wrap, trim ends, spread tops and sides with remaining whipped cream, leaving trimmed ends uncovered. Dust with a little sifted cocoa, if desired. Cut each tiramisu into 3 or 4 portions. Serve with liqueur custard and chocolate curls, if desired.

Liqueur Custard: Bring milk to boil in small pan. Whisk egg yolks, sugar and custard powder in small bowl until smooth. Whisk into milk, stir over heat, without boiling, until sauce thickens slightly. Stir in liqueur, press plastic over surface of custard; refrigerate until cold.

Serves 6 to 8.

- Tiramisu and liqueur custard can be made a day ahead.
- Storage: Covered, separately, in refrigerator.
- Freeze: Not suitable.
- Microwave: Chocolate and gelatine suitable.

Autumn Autumn Autumn Autumn Autumn Autumn Autumn Autumn Autumn

VANILLA CREAM CREPES WITH PORT WINE GRAPES

1 cup (150g) plain flour
2 teaspoons caster sugar
4 eggs
1½ cups (375ml) milk
2 tablespoons vegetable oil

VANILLA CREAM
1 cup (250ml) milk
½ cup (125ml) cream
1 vanilla bean
1 egg
2 egg yolks
2 tablespoons plain flour
⅓ cup (75g) caster sugar

PORT WINE GRAPES
1 cup (250ml) water
½ cup (125ml) redcurrant jelly
¼ cup (60ml) port wine
300g red grapes, halved

Sift flour and sugar into bowl, gradually stir in combined eggs, milk and oil; beat until smooth. Cover, stand 30 minutes.

Pour 2 tablespoons of batter into heated greased heavy-based crepe pan; cook until lightly browned underneath. Turn crepe, brown other side. Repeat with remaining batter. You need 16 crepes for this recipe. Cut crepes into 10cm rounds.

Just before serving, top half of each crepe with vanilla cream, fold crepe over to enclose filling. Serve crepes with port wine grapes and their syrup.

Vanilla Cream: Heat milk and cream in medium pan until almost boiling. Split vanilla bean in half lengthways; scrape seeds into small bowl, add egg, egg yolks, flour and sugar, whisk until creamy, gradually whisk into hot milk mixture. Stir over heat until mixture boils and thickens; press plastic over surface of custard, cool.

Port Wine Grapes: Combine water, jelly and wine in medium pan, stir over heat until jelly is melted. Simmer, uncovered, until reduced to about 1 cup (250ml). Add grapes, stir until heated through.

Serves 4 to 6.

▨ Can be prepared a day ahead.
▨ Storage: Covered, separately, in refrigerator.
▨ Freeze: Unfilled crepes suitable.
▨ Microwave: Vanilla cream suitable.

LEFT: Tiramisu with Liqueur Custard.
BELOW: Vanilla Cream Crepes with Port Wine Grapes.

Fabric from Boyac Decorative Furnishings

CAPE GOOSEBERRY SOUFFLE WITH ORANGE MUSCAT FRUIT

Any Sauternes-style dessert wine can be used instead of the orange muscat.

1 cup (250ml) water
1 cup (220g) caster sugar
1 cup (250ml) orange muscat dessert wine
1 cinnamon stick
1 vanilla bean
2 teaspoons grated orange rind
½ teaspoon ground ginger
800g cape gooseberries, halved
2 egg whites
1 tablespoon caster sugar, extra

Combine water, sugar, wine, cinnamon, vanilla bean, rind and ginger in medium pan, stir over heat, without boiling, until sugar is dissolved. Add gooseberries, simmer, uncovered, without stirring, 25 minutes.

Drain and reserve gooseberries and syrup in medium bowl. Push about ⅓ cup of the gooseberries through a fine sieve into another bowl. You need ¼ cup (60ml) puree; discard skins and seeds. Combine gooseberry puree with 1 tablespoon of reserved syrup.

Lightly grease 4 x ½ cup (125ml) souffle dishes, sprinkle base and sides evenly with a little caster sugar; shake away excess sugar. Place dishes on oven tray.

Beat egg whites in small bowl with electric mixer until soft peaks form, add extra sugar, beat until dissolved. Fold quarter of the egg white mixture into gooseberry puree, then fold in remaining egg whites. Spoon souffle mixture into dishes, level tops; bake in moderately hot oven about 10 minutes or until puffed and golden brown. Dust tops with a little extra sifted icing sugar, if desired. Serve immediately with reserved gooseberries and syrup.

Serves 4.

■ Souffles must be made just before serving. Gooseberry mixture can be made 3 days ahead.
■ Storage: Covered, in refrigerator.
■ Freeze: Not suitable.
■ Microwave: Not suitable.

China from Waterford Wedgwood

AVOCADO ICE-CREAM WITH MACADAMIA BREAD

2 large (640g) ripe avocados
1½ cups (375ml) thickened cream
1 cup (250ml) coconut cream
½ cup (125ml) maple syrup
¼ cup (40g) icing sugar mixture
1 tablespoon finely grated lemon rind
2 tablespoons lemon juice

MACADAMIA BREAD
2 egg whites
⅓ cup (75g) caster sugar
¾ cup (105g) plain flour
1 teaspoon vanilla essence
1½ cups (225g) macadamia nuts, toasted

Process avocados until smooth, add remaining ingredients, process until combined. Churn mixture in ice-cream maker following manufacturer's instructions. Spoon into plastic-wrap lined loaf pan, cover with foil, freeze until firm.

Remove ice-cream from freezer 15 minutes before serving, serve with macadamia bread.

Macadamia Bread: Lightly grease 8cm x 26cm bar pan, cover base and sides with baking paper. Beat egg whites in small bowl with electric mixer until soft peaks form, gradually add sugar, beating until dissolved between each addition. Fold in sifted flour, essence and nuts; spread mixture into prepared pan. Bake in moderate oven about 25 minutes or until lightly browned. Cool bread in pan, wrap in foil; stand overnight.

Using a serrated or electric knife, cut bread into 3mm slices. Place slices in single layer on oven trays. Bake in slow oven about 20 minutes or until crisp and dry; cool on wire rack.

Serves 6 to 8.

- Recipe can be made 4 days ahead.
- Storage: Ice-cream, covered, in freezer. Bread in airtight container.
- Freeze: Unsliced bread suitable.
- Microwave: Not suitable.

Bowl from Bondi Storehouse

LEFT: Avocado Ice-Cream with Macadamia Bread.
RIGHT: Quince Strudel.

QUINCE STRUDEL

3 medium (1kg) quinces
½ cup (110g) caster sugar
½ cup (125ml) water
1 vanilla bean
1 cinnamon stick
¼ teaspoon ground cinnamon
¼ teaspoon ground nutmeg
2 tablespoons packaged ground almonds
½ cup (60g) pecans, chopped
¼ cup (40g) sultanas
6 sheets fillo pastry
60g butter, melted
2 tablespoons packaged ground almonds, extra

Peel, core and thinly slice quinces. Combine with sugar, water, vanilla bean and cinnamon stick in medium pan, stir over heat, without boiling, until sugar is dissolved. Simmer, covered, about 20 minutes, stirring occasionally, until quinces are tender and pink. Drain, remove vanilla bean, discard cinnamon stick, cool.

Combine quinces, spices, nuts and sultanas in a medium bowl; mix gently. Layer fillo sheets together, brushing each with butter, and sprinkling with extra ground almonds.

Spoon filling 2cm from the edge of 1 long side, leaving 5cm at each end. Roll pastry from long side to enclose filling, tuck in ends. Place strudel on greased oven tray, brush with butter. Bake strudel in moderately hot oven for about 30 minutes or until lightly browned. Serve dusted with a little sifted icing sugar and cream, if desired.

Serves 4 to 6

- Best made just before serving. Quinces can be stewed a day ahead.
- Storage: Stewed quinces, covered, in refrigerator.
- Freeze: Not suitable.
- Microwave: Stewed quinces suitable.

PRICKLY PEAR SORBET WITH WAFER ROLLS

Use rubber gloves while peeling and chopping prickly pears.

8 (870g) pink prickly pears, peeled, chopped
3/4 cup (165g) caster sugar
2 cups (500ml) water
1/4 cup (60ml) orange juice
4 egg whites

WAFER ROLLS
2 egg whites
1/3 cup (75g) caster sugar
1/4 cup (35g) plain flour
1/4 teaspoon mixed spice
1/4 teaspoon ground ginger
40g butter, melted
1 teaspoon cinnamon sugar

Blend or process prickly pears until smooth, push through coarse sieve; discard seeds and pulp. Combine sugar and water in medium pan, stir over heat, without boiling, until sugar is dissolved. Simmer, uncovered, without stirring, 15 minutes; cool.

Stir pear puree and orange juice into sugar syrup, pour mixture into lamington pan, cover with foil, freeze until almost set.

Beat sorbet and egg whites in large bowl with electric mixer, or process, until smooth. Pour into loaf pan, cover, freeze until firm. Serve prickly pear sorbet with wafer rolls.

Wafer Rolls: Cook 1 or 2 trays of wafer rolls at a time for easy handling. Lightly grease 2 or 3 oven trays, cover with baking paper. Mark 4 x 8.5cm circles on baking paper.

Beat egg whites in small bowl with electric mixer until soft peaks form. Gradually add sugar, beat until dissolved, between additions. Fold in sifted flour and spices, then butter.

Drop rounded teaspoons of mixture into circles, spread evenly to fill circles. Sprinkle each circle with a pinch of cinnamon sugar. Bake in moderate oven about 6 minutes or until lightly browned.

Slide a metal spatula under 1 circle, quickly roll around a plastic chopstick, leave until firm. Repeat process with remaining circles.

Serves 6 to 8.

- Sorbet best made 2 days ahead. Wafer rolls best made on day of serving.
- Storage: Sorbet, covered, in freezer. Wafer rolls, in airtight container.
- Freeze: Wafer rolls not suitable.
- Microwave: Not suitable.

Plate setting from Dinosaur Designs

TAMARILLOS IN PORT SYRUP WITH SNOW EGGS

6 medium (660g) tamarillos
3 cups (660g) caster sugar
1/2 cup (125ml) port
3 cups (750ml) water
1 cinnamon stick
2 egg whites
1/3 cup (75g) caster sugar, extra

Cut shallow cross on base of each tamarillo, place in heatproof bowl, cover with boiling water, stand for 3 minutes. Rinse tamarillos under cold water, peel away skins.

Combine sugar, port, water and cinnamon in large pan, stir over heat, without boiling, until sugar is dissolved. Boil, uncovered, without stirring, about 10 minutes or until syrup thickens slightly. Add tamarillos, simmer, covered, about 15 minutes, or until tamarillos are just tender. Using a slotted spoon, place tamarillos in serving bowls; discard cinnamon stick, reserve syrup in pan.

Beat egg whites in small bowl with electric mixer until soft peaks form; gradually add extra sugar, beating until dissolved, between additions.

Working quickly, form heaped dessert-spoons of mixture into egg shapes.

Reheat syrup until just simmering. Using a spatula, gently push shaped egg-whites into barely simmering syrup. Cook about 3 or 4 snow eggs at a time.

Cook snow eggs 1 minute, turn carefully, cook further 1 minute. Using a slotted spoon, place snow eggs in serving bowls. Repeat with the remaining mixture. Strain syrup before serving with tamarillos and snow eggs.

Serves 6.

■ Best made just before serving.
■ Freeze: Not suitable.
■ Microwave: Not suitable.

ABOVE: Tamarillos in Port Syrup with Snow Eggs.
RIGHT: Guava Galette with Honey Ice-Cream.

GUAVA GALETTE WITH HONEY ICE-CREAM

1½ cups (225g) plain flour
185g cold butter, chopped
¼ cup (60ml) iced water, approximately
8 (1.2kg) guavas, peeled, halved
2 tablespoons caster sugar
½ cup (50g) pecans, toasted, ground
1 tablespoon plain flour, extra
1 teaspoon mixed spice
¼ cup (50g) firmly packed brown sugar
1 egg, lightly beaten

HONEY ICE-CREAM
2 cups (500ml) milk
8 egg yolks
2 tablespoons caster sugar
½ cup (125ml) honey
300ml thickened cream

Process flour and butter until combined. Add enough water to make ingredients just cling together. Knead dough on floured surface until smooth, roll out to a 40cm round, place on lightly greased oven tray. Cover, refrigerate 30 minutes or until firm.

Remove seeds from guavas, cut each half into 5 even slices. Combine caster sugar, nuts and extra flour in bowl; sprinkle over pastry, leaving a 6cm border. Place guava slices over nut mixture; sprinkle with combined spice and brown sugar. Fold pastry edge over filling, brush edge with egg. Bake in moderately hot oven about 50 minutes or until browned. Serve warm galette with honey ice-cream.

Honey Ice-Cream: Place milk in medium pan, bring to boil, remove from heat. Whisk egg yolks and sugar in small bowl until thick and pale, then gradually whisk into hot milk. Stir over heat, without boiling, about 15 minutes or until mixture thickens slightly; remove from heat; stir in honey. Pour mixture into large bowl. Cover surface with plastic wrap; cool. Refrigerate custard until cold.

Stir cream into custard, pour into deep 23cm square cake pan, cover with foil, freeze 3 hours or until just firm. Beat ice-cream in large bowl with electric mixer until smooth. Return ice-cream to cake pan, cover, freeze until firm.

Serves 6 to 8.

- Galette best made just before serving. Ice-cream best made a day ahead.
- Storage: Ice-cream, covered, in freezer.
- Freeze: Uncooked pastry suitable.
- Microwave: Not suitable.

Alessi plate from Ventura Designs; fabric from St James Furnishings

Winter

Family and friends will instantly warm to our heavenly puddings, cakes and luscious desserts as the chill of winter descends. Chocolate lovers will be head over heels for our truffle mud cake, souffles and rich chocolate caramel tart, and everyone will line up for seconds of the bread and butter puddings, the kumquat and almond dessert cake, and the tangelo tart.

CARAMELISED PEAR CREPES WITH SPIKED MASCARPONE

We used Frangelico in this recipe; use your favourite liqueur, if preferred.

6 medium (1kg) corella pears
30g butter
1/2 cup (100g) firmly packed brown sugar
2 tablespoons water
8 medium (200g) fresh dates, seeded, halved

CREPES
3/4 cup (105g) plain flour
3 eggs, lightly beaten
2 tablespoons vegetable oil
3/4 cup (180ml) milk

SPIKED MASCARPONE
1 cup (250g) mascarpone cheese
1/4 teaspoon ground cinnamon
1/4 teaspoon ground cardamom
1/4 teaspoon ground nutmeg
2 teaspoons icing sugar mixture
2 tablespoons Frangelico
1/3 cup (80ml) cream

Peel, quarter and core pears. Cut each quarter in half. Heat butter in large heavy-based pan, add pears, cook, stirring occasionally, about 10 minutes or until lightly browned. Add sugar, water and dates, stir gently until combined, simmer, stirring, about 3 minutes or until mixture thickens slightly. Serve hot pears and dates with folded crepes and spiked mascarpone.

Crepes: Sift flour into medium bowl, gradually whisk in combined eggs, oil and milk until smooth. Cover batter, stand 30 minutes.

Pour 2 to 3 tablespoons of batter into heated greased heavy-based crepe pan, cook until lightly browned underneath. Turn crepe, brown other side. Repeat with remaining batter. You will need 8 crepes for this recipe.

Spiked Mascarpone: Combine cheese, spices and sugar in bowl. Gradually stir in combined liqueur and cream.

Serves 4.

■ Crepes and spiked mascarpone can be made a day ahead. Pear and date mixture best made just before serving.
■ Storage: Crepes and mascarpone, covered, separately, in refrigerator.
■ Freeze: Crepes suitable.
■ Microwave: Not suitable.

CHOCOLATE LOVER'S TRUFFLE MUD CAKE

350g dark chocolate, chopped
250g unsalted butter, chopped
1 cup (250ml) water
1¼ cups (275g) caster sugar
2 cups (300g) plain flour
¼ cup (25g) cocoa powder
2 eggs, lightly beaten
50g dark chocolate, chopped, extra
¼ cup (60ml) apricot jam
15 chocolate-coated coffee beans

MODELLING CHOCOLATE
2 cups (300g) dark chocolate Melts
⅓ cup (80ml) light corn syrup
icing sugar mixture

CHOC-ORANGE TRUFFLES
¼ cup (60ml) cream
125g dark chocolate, chopped
1 tablespoon Kahlua or
  Creme de Cacao
¼ cup (35g) finely chopped
  pistachio nuts
1 teaspoon grated orange rind
¾ cup (125g) milk chocolate
  Melts, melted
¾ cup (125g) dark chocolate
  Melts, melted
1⅓ cups (200g) white chocolate
  Melts, melted
1 teaspoon shelled pistachio nuts,
  quartered, extra
1 teaspoon finely sliced orange rind

Grease deep 22cm round cake pan, cover base and side with baking paper. Combine chopped chocolate, butter, water and sugar in medium pan, stir over heat, without boiling, until chocolate is melted.

Sift flour and cocoa into large bowl. Whisk in warm chocolate mixture, then eggs, then extra chocolate. Pour mixture into prepared pan, bake in slow oven about 1¼ hours. Cool in pan. Cover cake, refrigerate overnight. Turn cake onto serving plate, brush with warmed strained jam. Dust cake with a little extra sifted cocoa, decorate with choc-orange truffles and chocolate-coated coffee beans.

Modelling Chocolate: Melt chocolate in small bowl, over hot water, add corn syrup, stir until mixture becomes thick and slightly grainy. Cover, stand about 3 hours or until mixture becomes firm.

Gently knead mixture on surface which has been lightly dusted with sifted icing sugar, until smooth and soft. Roll between sheets of baking paper into a round about 2mm thick and large enough to cover cake generously.

Place chocolate on cake, gently lifting and easing chocolate into decorative folds, press firmly around side of cake, trim edge.

Choc-Orange Truffles: Bring cream to boil in small pan, remove from heat, add chocolate; stir until melted. Mix in liqueur, nuts and grated rind, cover, refrigerate, stirring occasionally, about 30 minutes or until mixture thickens but is not set. Drop rounded teaspoons of mixture onto foil-covered tray, refrigerate about 1 hour or until firm.

Roll truffles into balls, refrigerate on tray until firm. Dip one-third of the truffles quickly into milk chocolate, gently and quickly roll between hands to coat evenly, return to tray. Repeat with half remaining truffles with dark chocolate and remaining truffles with white chocolate. Repeat dipping process with white chocolate-coated truffles for a good covering.

Use remaining melted chocolate to attach coffee beans, extra nuts or sliced orange rind to truffles; refrigerate truffles until set.

Serves 12.

- ▨ Mud cake and truffles best made a day ahead. Cake best assembled on day of serving.
- ▨ Storage: Covered, separately, in refrigerator.
- ▨ Freeze: Undecorated cake suitable.
- ▨ Microwave: Chocolate suitable.

Gold tray from Corso De' Fiori

APPLE TARTE TATIN

Golden delicious apples will give you the best results in this recipe.

2 tablespoons orange juice
2/3 cup (150g) caster sugar
70g unsalted butter
3 medium (450g) apples, peeled

PASTRY
1 cup (150g) plain flour
80g cold unsalted butter, chopped
1 tablespoon caster sugar
1 tablespoon cold water,
approximately

Combine juice, sugar and butter in 23cm heavy-based ovenproof frying pan, stir over heat, without boiling, until sugar is dissolved. Simmer, stirring occasionally, until mixture becomes a thick, light golden caramel. Remove from heat.

Halve apples; cut each half into 3 wedges, remove cores. Pack apple wedges tightly into pan over caramel, return to heat, simmer, uncovered, about 30 minutes or until most of the liquid is evaporated and caramel is dark golden brown. Remove from heat; cool 1 hour.

Roll pastry into a circle a little larger than the pan. Lift pastry, without stretching it, on top of apples, tuck in inside edge of pan. Bake in moderate oven about 25 minutes or until pastry is golden brown and crisp. Remove tarte from oven, stand 5 minutes. Carefully invert tarte onto plate. Serve warm with cream, if desired.

Pastry: Sift flour into bowl, rub in butter, stir in sugar. Add enough water to make ingredients just cling together. Knead dough on floured surface until smooth. Cover, refrigerate 1 hour.

Serves 6 to 8.

■ Apple caramel mixture and pastry can be made the day before.
■ Storage: Covered, separately, in refrigerator.
■ Freeze: Uncooked pastry suitable.
■ Microwave: Not suitable.

PERSIMMON RIPPLE ICE-CREAM

3 medium (900g) persimmons
1 2/3 cups (410ml) thickened cream
1 1/4 cups (310ml) milk
1/4 cup (60ml) honey
6 egg yolks
1/4 cup (55g) caster sugar

Peel persimmons; process flesh until smooth. Bring cream, milk and honey to boil in medium pan. Whisk egg yolks and sugar in medium bowl with electric mixer until creamy, gradually whisk into hot cream mixture. Stir over heat, without boiling, until mixture thickens slightly; remove from heat. Strain custard into 14cm x 21cm loaf pan, cover surface with plastic wrap, cool. Remove plastic, cover pan with foil, freeze until partly set.

Beat ice-cream in large bowl with electric mixer until smooth. Line same loaf pan with baking paper, pour in half the ice-cream mixture, swirl in 1/4 cup (60ml) persimmon puree. Pour in remaining ice-cream mixture, swirl in another 1/4 cup (60ml) persimmon puree; cover, freeze until set.

Turn ice-cream onto board, peel away paper, slice ice-cream and serve with remaining persimmon puree.

Serves 6.

■ Can be made 3 days ahead.
■ Storage: Covered, in freezer. Extra persimmon puree, covered, in refrigerator.
■ Microwave: Suitable.

China and cutlery from Villeroy & Boch; silver-frosted bowl from The Pacific East India Company

LEFT: Apple Tarte Tatin.
RIGHT: Persimmon Ripple Ice-Cream.

FIG AND ALMOND CAKE WITH BUTTERSCOTCH SAUCE

1½ cups (285g) chopped dried figs
1½ cups (375ml) water
1 teaspoon bicarbonate of soda
125g unsalted butter, softened
1 cup (220g) caster sugar
3 eggs
1 cup (150g) self-raising flour
½ cup (60g) packaged
    ground almonds
¼ cup (40g) finely chopped
    blanched almonds
300ml thickened cream

CHOCOLATE ALMOND WEDGES
¾ cup (100g) dark chocolate
    Melts, melted
¼ cup (20g) flaked
    almonds, toasted

BUTTERSCOTCH SAUCE
1 cup (200g) firmly packed
    brown sugar
1 cup (250ml) cream
150g unsalted butter
1 tablespoon Irish cream liqueur

Grease deep 22cm round cake pan, cover base with baking paper. Combine figs and water in pan, bring to boil, remove from heat, add soda, cover, stand 5 minutes. Blend or process until smooth.

Beat butter and sugar in small bowl with electric mixer until light and fluffy; beat in eggs 1 at a time. Transfer to large bowl, stir in sifted flour, both nuts, then warm fig mixture. Pour mixture into prepared pan, bake in moderate oven about 1 hour. Stand cake 10 minutes before turning onto wire rack to cool. Decorate cake with chocolate almond wedges and some of the whipped cream. Serve cake, sliced, with butterscotch sauce and remaining whipped cream.

Chocolate Almond Wedges: Mark a 21cm circle on baking-paper covered tray. Spread evenly with chocolate. Sprinkle edge with nuts.

When chocolate is almost set, cut into 12 wedges.

Butterscotch Sauce: Combine all ingredients in small pan, stir over heat, without boiling, until sugar is dissolved, simmer, without stirring for 3 minutes.

Serves 12.

■ Cake, chocolate almond wedges and butterscotch sauce can be made a day ahead.
■ Storage: Cake and chocolate wedges, in separate airtight containers. Sauce, covered, in refrigerator.
■ Freeze: Undecorated cake suitable.
■ Microwave: Figs, chocolate and sauce suitable.

Coffee cup from Caffe Bianchi

PASTRY-WRAPPED PEARS IN PORT

3 cups (660g) caster sugar
3 cups (750ml) water
1/2 cup (125ml) port
2 cinnamon sticks
4 large (1.3kg) pears, peeled
4 sheets ready-rolled puff pastry
1 egg, lightly beaten

Combine sugar, water, port and cinnamon in large pan, stir over heat, without boiling, until sugar is dissolved. Simmer uncovered, without stirring, about 30 minutes, or until syrup thickens slightly. Add pears (they should be a neat fit in the pan), simmer, covered, about 20 minutes or until pears are just tender. Cool pears in syrup.

Lift pears carefully from syrup. Drain on absorbent paper; reserve syrup. Trim pears so they sit upright.

Cut a 22cm circle from each sheet of pastry. Place pear in the centre of each pastry circle, draw edges together, fold excess pastry around pears. Brush lightly with egg, place on a greased oven tray, bake in moderate oven about 40 minutes or until golden. Serve pears hot with cream or ice-cream and some of the reserved syrup.

Serves 4.

▨ Pears can be cooked a day ahead. Recipe best made on day of serving.
▨ Storage: Covered, in refrigerator.
▨ Freeze: Not suitable.
▨ Microwave: Not suitable.

KUMQUAT JAM PUDDINGS WITH CUSTARD CREAM

350g kumquats
2 cups (500ml) water
1 cup (220g) caster sugar

CAKE MIXTURE
125g butter
1 teaspoon vanilla essence
1/2 cup (110g) caster sugar
2 eggs
2 cups (300g) self-raising flour
1/2 cup (125ml) milk

CUSTARD CREAM
3/4 cups (180ml) cream
3/4 cup (180ml) milk
4 egg yolks
1/4 cup (55g) caster sugar
2 tablespoons Grand Marnier or Cointreau

Grease 6 x 1 cup (250ml) ovenproof dishes. Cut kumquats into quarters lengthways, discard seeds. Combine kumquats and water in medium pan, simmer, uncovered, stirring occasionally, about 1 hour until kumquats are tender.

Add sugar to pan, stir over heat, without boiling, until sugar is dissolved. Simmer, uncovered, without stirring, about 10 minutes or until mixture is the consistency of a soft jam.

Divide kumquat mixture among dishes, top with cake mixture. Cover with greased foil, secure with string or rubber bands. Place dishes in large baking dish, pour in enough boiling water to come halfway up sides. Bake in moderate oven 30 minutes. Turn puddings onto serving plates, serve with custard cream.

Cake Mixture: Beat butter, essence and sugar in small bowl with electric mixer until thick and creamy, beat in eggs 1 at a time. Transfer mixture to medium bowl, stir in sifted flour and milk, in 2 batches.

Custard Cream: Bring cream and milk to boil in medium pan. Whisk egg yolks and sugar in medium bowl until thick and creamy, gradually whisk into hot milk mixture. Stir over heat, without boiling, until mixture thickens slightly; stir in liqueur.

Serves 6.

▨ Puddings best made just before serving. Kumquat mixture and custard cream can be made a day ahead.
▨ Storage: Kumquat mixture, covered, in cool, dry place. Custard, covered, in refrigerator.
▨ Freeze: Not suitable.
▨ Microwave: Not suitable.

OPPOSITE: Pastry-Wrapped Pears in Port.
ABOVE: Kumquat Jam Puddings with Custard Cream.

WONDERFUL WEDDING CAKE

This mud cake is a delicious and popular alternative to a traditional fruit cake. Cut in small (3cm) squares, the cake will serve 60 to 80 guests.

It can be prepared 2 weeks ahead; store uniced cake in airtight container in refrigerator. Uniced cake can also be frozen for up to 3 months. The cake is not suitable to microwave.

If ivory paste colour is unavailable, use equal quantities of egg-yellow and caramel liquid colours.

The decorated cake, without flowers, can be made 3 days ahead; keep in a cool, dry place but do not refrigerate. Purchase fresh flowers; check which varieties last the longest – once cut, they will remain fresh for several hours before serving time. Silk flowers could also be used.

RICH CHOCOLATE MUD CAKE

1.2kg dark cooking chocolate, chopped
750g butter
1/3 cup dry instant coffee
2 1/4 cups (560ml) water
2 1/4 cups (450g) firmly packed brown sugar
3 cups (450g) plain flour
3/4 cup (110g) self-raising flour
6 eggs, lightly beaten
3/4 cup (180ml) Creme de Cacao, Kahlua or Tia Maria

Grease a deep 17cm round cake pan and a deep 25cm round cake pan; cover bases and sides of each pan with 3 layers of baking paper.

Combine chocolate, butter, coffee, water and sugar in large pan, stir over heat, without boiling, until chocolate is melted.

Sift flours into large bowl, stir in warm chocolate mixture, then combined eggs and liqueur. Pour 1/3 of the mixture into prepared small pan, pour remaining mixture into prepared large pan. Bake cakes in moderately slow oven about 2 1/2 hours for small cake and about 3 1/2 hours for large cake. Cover cakes loosely with baking paper after 1 hour to prevent overbrowning. Cool cakes in pans. Turn cakes from pans, remove paper. Wrap cakes in plastic wrap, refrigerate.

DECORATIONS

Cake boards can be purchased ready-covered with special non-absorbent paper from cake decorators' suppliers or health food stores. If unavailable, they can be made from masonite or similar material. Cover boards with cake decorators' paper, glossy gift paper or foil-coated paper. We have covered the cakes with fondant while on the boards. If preferred, you can fondant-cover the cakes on baking paper then transfer them to the boards when the fondant is firm.

36cm round board
50cm coloured fabric
fabric glue
16cm round board
2 tablespoons apricot jam, warmed, strained
1kg packaged fondant (soft icing)
pure icing sugar
ivory concentrated paste food colouring
5 butchers' wooden skewers
3 cups (450g) white chocolate Melts, melted
2 tablespoons vegetable oil
red food colouring
1 cup (150g) white chocolate Melts, melted, extra
4.5m ribbon
50cm fine wire
parafilm tape (available from florists)
fresh or silk flowers

Cover 36cm board with fabric or paper, secure with glue. Cover 16cm board on both sides with paper, secure with glue. Invert cakes onto prepared boards; brush crumbs away, brush cakes evenly with jam.

Knead fondant until smooth on surface dusted with sifted icing sugar. Knead in enough ivory colouring to reach shade desired. Cut off 2/3 of fondant, wrap remaining piece tightly in plastic wrap. Roll fondant on surface dusted with sifted icing sugar until large enough to cover top and side of large cake.

Lift fondant over cake then lightly mould fondant onto cake with icing-sugared hands; trim edge neatly. Cover small cake in same way with remaining fondant. Stand cakes at room temperature for about 6 hours or until the fondant has developed a slight crust.

Push pointed ends of skewers into large cake; remove skewers, then push skewers into cake, blunt end first. Mark skewers level with top of cake. Remove skewers, cut with serrated knife; push skewers back into cake.

Position small cake, on its board, on skewers in centre of large cake.

Cut 4 pieces of baking paper, 2 measuring 9cm x 48cm and 2 measuring 9cm x 36cm. Combine chocolate with oil, tint with ivory colouring and a little red colouring, to match fondant. Spread chocolate mixture evenly over paper; stand at room temperature until set. Cut chocolate into 4cm pieces.

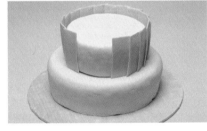

Spread a little of the extra chocolate on back of each chocolate piece, overlap chocolate pieces around edge of cakes. Secure ribbon around cakes with a little of the extra chocolate. Tie bows, secure with glue to ribbon. Make ribbon loops for top of cake, secure with wire, cover wire with tape, place on top of cake. Decorate with flowers.

STICKY CHOCOLATE DATE PUDDING

1½ cups (240g) seeded chopped dates
1¾ cups (430ml) water
1 teaspoon bicarbonate of soda
80g butter, chopped
⅔ cup (150g) caster sugar
2 eggs
1 cup (150g) self-raising flour
⅓ cup (35g) cocoa powder
⅔ cup (70g) pecans, toasted, chopped

BUTTERSCOTCH SAUCE
1¼ cups (250g) firmly packed brown sugar
80g butter
300ml thickened cream

CHOCOLATE HEARTS
1 cup (150g) dark chocolate Melts, melted

Grease deep 22cm round cake pan, cover base with baking paper. Combine dates and water in small pan, bring to boil, remove from heat, add soda, cover, stand 5 minutes. Blend or process until smooth.

Beat butter and sugar in small bowl with electric mixer until combined, beat in eggs quickly, 1 at a time. Transfer mixture to large bowl, fold in sifted flour and cocoa, then add nuts, with warm date mixture, in 2 batches. Pour mixture into prepared pan, bake in moderate oven about 1 hour. Stand pudding 10 minutes before turning onto serving plate. Serve pudding with hot butterscotch sauce and chocolate hearts, and whipped cream, if desired.

Butterscotch Sauce: Combine all ingredients in medium pan, stir over heat, without boiling, until sugar is dissolved then simmer, without stirring, 3 minutes.

Chocolate Hearts: Cover oven tray with baking paper, spread evenly with chocolate. When chocolate is almost set, cut into 4cm heart shapes. When chocolate is completely set, lift hearts from paper with metal spatula.

Serves 8 to 10.

■ Can be made several days ahead.
■ Storage: Pudding and hearts, in separate airtight containers. Sauce, covered, in refrigerator.
■ Freeze: Pudding suitable.
■ Microwave: Dates, sauce and chocolate suitable.

Plate from Villeroy & Boch

RHUBARB FILLO PARCELS WITH HAZELNUT SAUCE

You will need about 10 stalks of rhubarb for this recipe.

30g butter
6 cups chopped rhubarb
½ cup (100g) firmly packed brown sugar
10 sheets fillo pastry
50g butter, melted, extra
1 cup (100g) plain cake crumbs
1 cup (150g) roasted hazelnuts, finely chopped

HAZELNUT SAUCE
1 vanilla bean
1 cup (250ml) milk
1 cup (250ml) cream
6 egg yolks
½ cup (110g) caster sugar
2 tablespoons Frangelico

Melt butter in pan, add rhubarb, cook, stirring occasionally, about 5 minutes or until rhubarb is just soft. Add sugar, cook, stirring, without boiling, until sugar is dissolved; cool.

Layer 5 sheets of pastry, brushing each layer with extra butter. Cut layered sheets in half, crossways. Place ½ cup of the combined crumbs and nuts in centre of each piece of pastry, top with quarter of the rhubarb mixture. Bring edges of pastry together in centre, press firmly to seal. Repeat with remaining pastry, butter, hazelnut and rhubarb mixture. Place parcels on greased oven tray, bake in moderately hot oven about 15 minutes or until browned. Serve with hazelnut sauce.

Hazelnut Sauce: Split vanilla bean in half lengthways. Bring milk, cream and vanilla bean to boil in medium pan; remove bean. Whisk egg yolks and sugar in medium bowl until creamy, gradually whisk into hot milk mixture. Stir over heat, without boiling, until mixture thickens slightly; stir in liqueur.

Serves 4.

- Filling and sauce can be made a day ahead. Parcels best made just before serving.
- Storage: Covered, separately, in refrigerator.
- Freeze: Not suitable.
- Microwave: Not suitable.

KUMQUAT AND ALMOND DESSERT CAKE

600g kumquats
2 cups (320g) blanched
    almonds, toasted
6 eggs
1 cup (220g) caster sugar
¼ cup (40g) semolina
1 teaspoon baking powder

CREME ANGLAISE
1¾ cups (430ml) milk
4 egg yolks
¼ cup (55g) caster sugar
1 teaspoon vanilla essence

Grease 24cm springform tin, cover base with baking paper. Sprinkle sides of tin with a little flour; shake away excess flour, stand tin on oven tray. Add whole kumquats to pan of boiling water; simmer, covered, 1 hour or until very soft; drain.

Halve kumquats, discard seeds, blend or process kumquats until smooth. Process almonds until finely chopped. Beat eggs and sugar in medium bowl with electric mixer until pale and thick. Fold in kumquat puree, almonds, semolina and sifted baking powder. Pour mixture into prepared tin, bake in moderate oven about 1 hour. Stand cake 10 minutes, turn onto wire rack to cool. Serve dusted with sifted icing sugar, if desired, and creme anglaise.

Creme Anglaise: Bring milk to boil in medium pan. Whisk egg yolks and sugar in medium bowl until creamy, gradually whisk into hot milk. Stir over heat, without boiling, until mixture thickens slightly; stir in essence.

Serves 6 to 8.

- Cake can be made 3 days ahead.
- Storage: Cake in airtight container; creme anglaise, covered in refrigerator.
- Freeze: Cake suitable.
- Microwave: Not suitable.

OPPOSITE: Rhubarb Fillo Parcels with Hazelnut Sauce. BELOW: Kumquat and Almond Dessert Cake.

Winter Winter Winter Winter Winter Winter Winter Winter Winter Winter Winter Winter Winter

CHOCOLATE-BROWNIE CARAMEL TART

1 cup (150g) plain flour
100g cold unsalted butter, chopped
1/4 cup (55g) caster sugar
1/2 cup (75g) finely chopped macadamia nuts
1 egg yolk
icing sugar mixture

CARAMEL FILLING
60g unsalted butter
400g can sweetened condensed milk
1 tablespoon golden syrup
2 tablespoons cream

CHOCOLATE-BROWNIE TOPPING
80g unsalted butter
1/2 cup (110g) caster sugar
70g dark chocolate, chopped
1 egg, lightly beaten
1/4 cup (35g) plain flour
1 tablespoon cocoa powder

Grease 24cm round loose-based flan tin. Process flour and butter until crumbly, add sugar, nuts and egg yolk, process until ingredients just cling together. Knead dough gently on floured surface until smooth. Press dough over base and side of prepared tin, prick base with fork, cover, refrigerate 30 minutes.

Cover pastry with baking paper large enough to extend 10cm over edge, tuck paper under tin to completely cover pastry, fill with dried beans or rice. Place tin on oven tray, bake in moderately hot oven 15 minutes, remove beans and paper, loosely cover top edge of pastry with greased foil, bake further 8 minutes or until pastry is lightly browned; cool.

Spread warm caramel filling into pastry case, stand 30 minutes or until cold and firm. Pour chocolate-brownie topping over caramel, bake in moderate oven about 40 minutes. Cool in tin, cover, refrigerate 4 hours or overnight before serving.

Using cardboard or thick paper, cut out 6 x 5cm heart-shaped templates. Place templates around tart, dust top of tart with sifted icing sugar; carefully remove templates. Serve tart with whipped cream, if desired.

Caramel Filling: Combine all ingredients in small pan, cook, stirring, over medium heat about 10 minutes, until caramel becomes golden brown. Allow to cool slightly before attempting to spread.

Chocolate-Brownie Topping: Melt butter in small pan, add sugar, stir over heat, without boiling, until sugar is dissolved. Remove from heat, add chocolate, stir until melted, then stir in egg, sifted flour and cocoa; cool.

Serves 8 to 10.

■ Best made a day ahead.
■ Storage: Covered, in refrigerator.
■ Freeze: Not suitable.
■ Microwave: Not suitable.

Cake stand from H.A.G. Imports

MANDARIN, RICOTTA AND CHOCOLATE TART

3 medium (250g) mandarins
90g butter, softened
¼ cup (55g) caster sugar
1 egg
1¼ cups (185g) plain flour
¼ cup (35g) self-raising flour
¼ cup (60ml) orange marmalade,
  warmed

FILLING
2 egg yolks
¼ cup (55g) caster sugar
2¼ cups (450g) ricotta cheese
80g dark chocolate, grated

Finely grate rind from mandarins. You need 2 tablespoons rind for the filling. Peel mandarins, break into segments.

Beat butter, sugar and egg in small bowl with electric mixer, until just combined. Stir in half the sifted flours, mix remaining flours into dough by hand. Knead dough on floured surface, until just smooth; do not over-handle. Wrap in plastic, refrigerate 30 minutes.

Roll pastry between sheets of baking paper until piece is large enough to line 10cm x 34cm rectangular loose-based flan tin. Cover, refrigerate 30 minutes.

Cover pastry with baking paper, fill with dried beans or rice, place on oven tray, bake in moderately hot oven 10 minutes, remove beans and paper; cool.

Spoon filling into pastry case, top with mandarin segments. Bake in moderate oven about 35 minutes or until just set. Brush tart with strained marmalade; stand 5 minutes before serving.

Filling: Beat egg yolks and sugar in small bowl with electric mixer until thick and pale. Beat in cheese, then stir in chocolate and reserved rind.

Serves 4 to 6.

- Can be made a day ahead.
- Storage: Covered, in refrigerator.
- Freeze: Uncooked pastry suitable.
- Microwave: Marmalade suitable.

Tiles and plate from Country Floors

CHOCOLATE CHECKERBOARD CAKE

125g butter
3/4 cup (100g) dark
    chocolate Melts
3/4 cup (180ml) water
1 cup (200g) firmly packed
    brown sugar
1 tablespoon dry instant coffee
3/4 cup (105g) self-raising flour
1/2 cup (75g) plain flour
1/3 cup (35g) cocoa powder
2 eggs

MILK CHOCOLATE CAKE
125g butter
3/4 cup (100g) milk
    chocolate Melts
3/4 cup (180ml) water
1 cup (220g) caster sugar
1 cup (150g) self-raising flour
1/2 cup (75g) plain flour
2 eggs

GLAZE
3/4 cup (180ml) apricot jam
2 teaspoons gelatine

CHOCOLATE GANACHE
1 1/3 cup (180g) dark
    chocolate Melts
60g unsalted butter

CREME ANGLAISE
2 1/2 cups (625ml) milk
6 egg yolks
1/4 cup (55g) caster sugar
2 teaspoons vanilla essence

Grease deep 19cm square cake pan, cover base and sides with baking paper. Combine butter, chocolate, water, sugar and coffee in small pan, stir over heat, without boiling, until chocolate is melted. Transfer mixture to large bowl, add sifted dry ingredients, beat with electric mixer until combined. Add eggs 1 at a time, beat until combined. Pour mixture into prepared pan, bake in moderately slow oven about 45 minutes. Stand cake 5 minutes before turning onto wire rack to cool.
Milk Chocolate Cake: Use method above for making this cake.

Trim both cakes to perfect squares.

Cut cakes into 5 even strips.

Cover a tray with baking paper. When ready to assemble cake, brush cake strips with glaze.

Join glazed strips as shown.

Spread cake with chocolate ganache. Serve sliced, with creme anglaise.
Glaze: Combine jam and gelatine in small pan, stir over heat, without boiling, until gelatine is dissolved; strain.
Chocolate Ganache: Melt chocolate and butter in heatproof bowl over pan of simmering water. Cool to room temperature. Beat with wooden spoon until mixture is thick and spreadable.
Creme Anglaise: Bring milk to boil in medium pan. Whisk egg yolks and sugar in medium bowl until creamy, gradually whisk into hot milk. Stir over heat, without boiling, until mixture thickens slightly; stir in essence.

Serves 6 to 8.

- Can be prepared a day ahead.
- Storage: Cake in airtight container. Creme anglaise, covered, in refrigerator.
- Freeze: Not suitable.
- Microwave: Glaze and ganache suitable.

SPICED DATE PUDDINGS WITH CARAMEL SAUCE

You need 350g fresh dates for this recipe.

11 medium (250g) fresh dates, seeded, chopped
3/4 cup (180ml) water
1/2 teaspoon bicarbonate of soda
50g butter
1/3 cup (65g) firmly packed brown sugar
1 egg
1/2 cup (75g) self-raising flour
1 teaspoon ground cardamom
1/2 teaspoon ground ginger
1/2 teaspoon ground cinnamon
pinch ground cloves
1/2 medium (75g) apple, peeled, cored, quartered
4 medium (90g) fresh dates, seeded, sliced, extra
1 tablespoon golden syrup

CARAMEL SAUCE
3/4 cup (150g) firmly packed brown sugar
300ml thickened cream
100g butter
1/3 cup (80ml) milk
2 tablespoons Kahlua

Grease 4 x 2/3 cup (160ml) ovenproof dishes. Combine chopped dates and water in pan, bring to boil, remove from heat, add soda; cover, stand 5 minutes. Process mixture until smooth.

Beat butter, sugar and egg in small bowl with electric mixer until thick and creamy. Stir in sifted flour and spices, then warm date mixture. Pour mixture into prepared dishes to come 2/3 of way up sides of dishes. Press an apple quarter into each pudding mixture, spoon remaining mixture over apples.

Cut 4 x 15cm square sheets of baking paper and foil. Layer 1 sheet of baking paper and 1 of foil together, fold a 2cm pleat in centre; place paper side down over puddings, secure with string. Place puddings on oven tray, bake in moderately slow oven 40 minutes. Stand puddings, covered, for 5 minutes. Turn puddings onto serving plates; top with extra sliced dates, drizzle with golden syrup and serve with caramel sauce.

Caramel Sauce: Combine sugar, cream and butter in medium pan, stir over heat, without boiling, until sugar is dissolved, simmer, without stirring, for 3 minutes. Stir in milk and liqueur.

Serves 4.

■ Can be made a day ahead.
■ Storage: Covered, separately, in refrigerator.
■ Freeze: Puddings suitable.
■ Microwave: Dates and sauce suitable.

Plates, cups and saucers from Villeroy & Boch; fabric from Boyac Decorative Furnishings

Plate, spoon and eggcup from Villeroy & Boch; fabric from South Pacific Fabrics

HOT CHOCOLATE SOUFFLES WITH LIQUEUR CREAM

2 tablespoons caster sugar
1 tablespoon cornflour
1 tablespoon plain flour
1/2 cup (110g) caster sugar, extra
1/2 cup (125ml) milk
1/3 cup (35g) cocoa powder
1 tablespoon dry instant coffee
4 eggs, separated
2 egg whites

LIQUEUR CREAM
1 1/2 cups (375g) mascarpone cheese
2 tablespoons icing sugar mixture
1/4 cup (60ml) Kahlua

Grease 8 x 3/4 cup (180ml) ovenproof dishes. Sprinkle base and sides with sugar; shake away excess sugar. Place dishes on oven tray. Blend flours and extra sugar with some of the milk in small pan, whisk in remaining milk, whisk over heat until mixture boils and thickens; remove from heat. Whisk in combined cocoa and coffee until dissolved. Whisk in egg yolks; transfer mixture to large bowl.

Beat egg whites in small bowl with electric mixer until firm peaks form. Fold about 1/4 of the egg whites into chocolate mixture then fold in remaining whites. Spoon mixture into prepared dishes, bake in moderately hot oven about 20 minutes or until souffles are puffed. Serve souffles immediately,

with liqueur cream, and sprinkled with a little sifted cocoa, if desired.

Liqueur Cream: Beat all ingredients in small bowl with whisk or electric mixer until just combined.

Serves 8.

- Souffles must be made just before serving. Liqueur cream can be made a day ahead.
- Storage: Covered, in refrigerator.
- Freeze: Not suitable.
- Microwave: Not suitable.

LEFT: Spiced Date Puddings with Caramel Sauce.
ABOVE: Hot Chocolate Souffles with Liqueur Cream.

CITRUS ALMOND SYRUP CAKE

2 medium (360g) oranges
1½ cups (240g) almond kernels
1 cup (220g) caster sugar
6 eggs
1 teaspoon baking powder
1 teaspoon vanilla essence

LIME SYRUP
½ cup (110g) caster sugar
¼ cup (60ml) lime juice
¼ cup (60ml) water

Place whole oranges in medium pan, add enough hot water to cover oranges. Cover, bring to boil, then simmer about 2 hours, or until oranges are tender. Replenish water with boiling water as it evaporates during cooking. Drain oranges, cool; discard water.

Grease deep 20cm round cake pan, cover base with baking paper. Process almonds and sugar until almonds are roughly chopped; transfer mixture to medium bowl. Quarter whole oranges, blend or process until smooth.

With motor operating, add eggs 1 at a time, process until combined. Add almond mixture, baking powder and essence, process until just combined. Spread mixture into prepared pan. Bake in moderately slow oven about 1 hour. Pour hot lime syrup over hot cake. Stand cake in pan for 30 minutes. Turn cake onto wire rack over tray. Serve warm or cold with caramelised orange and lime rind, if desired.

Lime Syrup: Combine all ingredients in small pan, stir over heat, without boiling, until sugar is dissolved. Simmer, uncovered, without stirring, about 5 minutes or until slightly thickened.

Serves 6 to 8.

- Can be made a day ahead.
- Storage: In airtight container.
- Freeze: Not suitable.
- Microwave: Not suitable.

Cake stand from The Bay Tree Kitchen Shop

BROWNIES WITH HOT FUDGE SAUCE AND ICE-CREAM

250g unsalted butter
250g dark chocolate, chopped
2½ cups (550g) caster sugar
5 eggs
1 teaspoon vanilla essence
⅔ cup (100g) plain flour
⅓ cup (50g) self-raising flour
½ cup (50g) cocoa powder
50g dark chocolate, chopped, extra

ICE-CREAM
1 vanilla bean
2½ cups (625ml) milk
6 egg yolks
¾ cup (165g) caster sugar
1 tablespoon custard powder
300ml thickened cream

HOT FUDGE SAUCE
½ cup (125ml) cream
150g dark chocolate, chopped
10 (50g) white marshmallows, chopped

Grease 20cm x 30cm lamington pan, cover base and sides with baking paper.

Combine butter and chocolate in medium pan, stir over low heat until smooth; transfer to large bowl. Stir in sugar, then eggs and essence, then sifted flours and cocoa and extra chocolate. Pour mixture into prepared pan. Bake in moderate oven for about 45 minutes or until firm; cool in pan. Refrigerate until cold. Turn brownie onto board, trim edges, cut into quarters; cut each quarter in half diagonally, cut each triangle in half. Serve brownies with ice-cream and hot fudge sauce.

Ice-Cream: Split vanilla bean in half lengthways, combine with milk in medium pan, bring to boil, remove from heat, cover, stand 10 minutes; strain. Discard vanilla bean.

Bring the milk back to boil in same pan. Whisk egg yolks, sugar and custard powder in medium bowl until well-combined, gradually whisk into hot milk. Stir over heat, without boiling, until mixture thickens slightly. Press plastic over surface of custard, cool to room temperature. Fold in whipped cream. Churn mixture in ice-cream maker following manufacturer's instructions. Spoon ice-cream into deep 19cm square cake pan, cover with foil, freeze until firm.

Hot Fudge Sauce: Combine all ingredients in small pan, stir over heat, without boiling, until smooth.

Serves 8.

■ Recipe can be made a day ahead.
■ Storage: Brownies and sauce, covered, separately, in refrigerator.
■ Freeze: Brownies suitable.
■ Microwave: Sauce suitable.

Plates from Waterford Wedgwood; spoon from Victoria Spring Designs

HEAVENLY BREAD AND BUTTER PUDDINGS

12 slices raisin bread
60g butter
2/3 cup (110g) seeded prunes, sliced
1/4 cup (35g) finely chopped dried apricots
ground nutmeg

CUSTARD
2 eggs
1/2 cup (125ml) milk
1/2 cup (125ml) cream
1/4 cup (55g) caster sugar
1 tablespoon Grand Marnier

CITRUS SAUCE
1/2 cup (125ml) marmalade
1/2 cup (125ml) water
1 tablespoon Grand Marnier
100g butter

Lightly grease 4 x 3/4 cup (180ml) souffle dishes; cover bases with baking paper. Cut bread into 12 x 8.5cm rounds, spread both sides of bread with butter. Toast bread on both sides.

Place toast rounds in base of each dish, top with half the prunes and half the apricots. Repeat layering with toast, prunes and apricots; finishing with toast. Place dishes in baking dish. Slowly pour custard into dishes, stand 5 minutes or until custard is absorbed.

Pour enough boiling water into baking dish to come halfway up side of souffle dishes. Bake, uncovered, in moderately slow oven about 30 minutes or until puddings are just set.

Run a thin-bladed knife around outside of puddings, turn puddings onto oven tray, remove baking paper. Using large spatula, turn puddings over,

brush tops with citrus sauce, lightly sprinkle tops with nutmeg. Brown puddings under hot grill; serve with citrus sauce.

Custard: Whisk all ingredients in jug until combined.

Citrus Sauce: Combine all ingredients in medium pan, stir over heat, without boiling, until marmalade is melted, then simmer, stirring, about 3 minutes or until sauce thickens slightly; strain.

Serves 4.

■ Best made close to serving.
■ Freeze: Not suitable.
■ Microwave: Not suitable.

TANGELO AND HAZELNUT TART

You need about 3 (650g) tangelos for this recipe.

1 cup (110g) packaged
   ground hazelnuts
80g cold butter, chopped
2 tablespoons icing sugar mixture
2 tablespoons plain flour

FILLING
6 egg yolks
2 egg whites
3/4 cup (180ml) cream
1/2 cup (110g) caster sugar
1 tablespoon finely grated
   tangelo rind
1/4 cup (60ml) strained tangelo juice
2 tablespoons Franjelico

CARAMELISED RIND
2 tangelos
2 cups (500ml) water
1 cup (220g) caster sugar

Process hazelnuts, butter, sugar and flour until ingredients just cling together. Use floured fingers to press hazelnut mixture over base and side of 23cm round loose-based flan tin; refrigerate 30 minutes.

Place flan tin on oven tray, prick base of pastry all over with fork, bake in moderate oven 15 minutes. Lightly press base of pastry case with back of spoon to flatten, bake another 5 minutes; cool.

Pour filling into pastry case, bake in slow oven about 40 minutes or until filling is almost set in centre; cool. Gently loosen tart from side of tin; cover, refrigerate until cold. Serve tart with caramelised rind and a little syrup.

Filling: Whisk all ingredients together in a large jug; stand 5 minutes to allow air bubbles to subside.

Caramelised Rind: Use a vegetable peeler to peel rind thinly from tangelos. Cut rind into thin strips. Combine water and sugar in small pan, stir over heat, without boiling, until sugar is dissolved. Add rind, simmer, uncovered, without stirring, about 15 minutes or until rind is slightly caramelised; cool.

Serves 8 to 10.

- Best made a day ahead.
- Storage: Tart and rind in syrup, covered, separately, in refrigerator.
- Freeze: Not suitable.
- Microwave: Not suitable.

OPPOSITE: Heavenly Bread and Butter Puddings. RIGHT: Tangelo and Hazelnut Tart.

Plates from Dinosaur Designs

APPLE CHARLOTTE

We used metal charlotte moulds, but souffle dishes can be used instead.

6 medium (900g) apples, peeled, cored, chopped
1 teaspoon grated lemon rind
1 tablespoon lemon juice
½ teaspoon ground cinnamon
¼ teaspoon ground nutmeg
¼ cup (55g) caster sugar
¼ cup (60ml) water
13 slices white bread
100g unsalted butter, melted
¼ cup (80ml) apricot jam
2 tablespoons water, extra

QUICK CINNAMON CUSTARD
¼ teaspoon ground cinnamon
¾ cup (180ml) prepared pouring custard
2 tablespoons milk

Combine apples, rind, juice, cinnamon, nutmeg, sugar and water in large pan; simmer, stirring occasionally, about 10 minutes or until apples are tender; cool, strain.

Remove crusts from bread slices. Cut 2 x 5.5cm rounds from each of 2 slices; cut remaining 11 slices into 3 strips each. Grease 4 x 1cup (250ml) ovenproof moulds. Brush both sides of bread with butter, place rounds in base of each mould.

Line sides of moulds with bread strips, slightly overlapping edges, extending bread 1.5cm above top edge of mould. Pack apple mixture firmly into moulds.

Fold bread toward centre to cover filling, press firmly to seal. Place moulds on oven tray, bake, uncovered, in moderately hot oven about 35 minutes or until bread is golden brown. Stand charlottes 10 minutes before turning out of moulds onto serving plates.

Place jam and extra water in small pan, simmer, stirring occasionally, about 5 minutes or until glaze is thickened slightly. Strain glaze, brush over charlottes. Serve warm charlottes with quick cinnamon custard.

Quick Cinnamon Custard: Combine all ingredients in small jug; mix well.

Serves 4.

- Charlottes best made close to serving. Quick cinnamon custard can be made a day ahead.
- Storage: Covered, in refrigerator.
- Freeze: Not suitable.
- Microwave: Glaze suitable.

China and cutlery from The Bay Tree Kitchen Shop

Rhubarb

Guavas

Glossary

Here are some terms, names and alternatives to help
everyone use and understand our recipes perfectly.

Cashews

ALCOHOL: see Liqueurs, Sauternes.

ALLSPICE: pimento.

AMARETTI BISCUITS: small Italian-style macaroons based on ground almonds.

ARROWROOT: used mostly for thickening. Cornflour can be substituted but will not give as clear a glaze.

BAKING PAPER: also known as parchment, silicon paper or non-stick baking paper; not to be confused with greaseproof. Used to line pans but can also be used to make piping bags.

BAKING POWDER: a raising agent consisting mainly of cream of tartar and bicarbonate of soda in the proportions of 2:1; the equivalent of 2 teaspoons baking powder is 1 level teaspoon cream of tartar to 1/2 level teaspoon bicarbonate of soda.

BICARBONATE OF SODA: baking soda.

BISCUIT: cookie.

BRIOCHE: rich French yeast bread made with butter and eggs available from specialised French or better breadshops.

Blanched almonds

BUTTER: use salted or unsalted (also called sweet) butter; 125g is equal to 1 stick butter.

BUTTERMILK: is made by adding a culture to a low-fat milk to give a slightly sour taste; low-fat yogurt can be substituted, if preferred.

BUTTERNUT COOKIES: biscuits made from sugar, flour, rolled oats, butter, coconut and golden syrup.

CARAMBOLA: also known as star fruit; five-cornered, pale golden-yellow, crisp and juicy fruit with a waxy edible skin.

CHEESE:

Cream: also known as Philly.

Mascarpone: a fresh, thick, triple-cream cheese with a delicately sweet, slightly sour taste.

Quark: a fresh soft cheese made from skim milk with a mildly sour taste.

Ricotta: a fresh, sweet, fairly moist curd cheese.

CHOCOLATE:

Compounded: for dipping and coating.

Dark: eating chocolate.

Dark cooking: we used premium quality dark cooking rather than compounded.

Dark Melts: for melting and moulding.

Milk: primarily for eating.

White Melts: for melting and moulding.

CINNAMON SUGAR: combination of caster sugar and ground cinnamon.

COCOA: cocoa powder.

COCONUT: use desiccated coconut unless otherwise specified.

Cream: available in cans and cartons; is made from coconut and water.

Whole fresh: choose coconut that is heavy for its size; shake to make certain it contains liquid. This liquid should not be confused with coconut milk.

CORNFLOUR: cornstarch.

CORN SYRUP: an imported product. It is available in light or dark colour; either can be substituted for the other; glucose syrup (liquid glucose) can be substituted.

CREAM (minimum fat content 35%): fresh pouring cream.

Rich (minimum fat content 54%): thick, not suitable for whipping.

Sour (minimum fat content 35%): a thick commercially cultured soured cream.

Thickened (minimum fat content 35%): a whipping cream that contains a thickener.

CREAM OF TARTAR: an ingredient in baking powder. It is also sometimes added to confectionery mixtures to help prevent sugar from crystallising.

CUSTARD POWDER: vanilla pudding mix.

CUSTARD, PREPARED: pouring custard, available in cartons.

DESSERT NOUGAT: we used Callard & Bowser dessert nougat.

Almond kernels

Flaked almonds

Pomegranates

Brazil nuts

Corella pears

Fresh dates

Lychees

Tangelos

Large orange paw paw

Whole small red paw paw

Red paw paw

Passionfruit

Persimmons

Strawberries

Blackberries

Blueberries

Raspberries

Boysenberries

Rockmelon

Honeydew melon

Watermelon

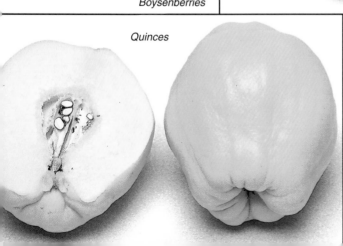
Quinces

Black figs

Green figs

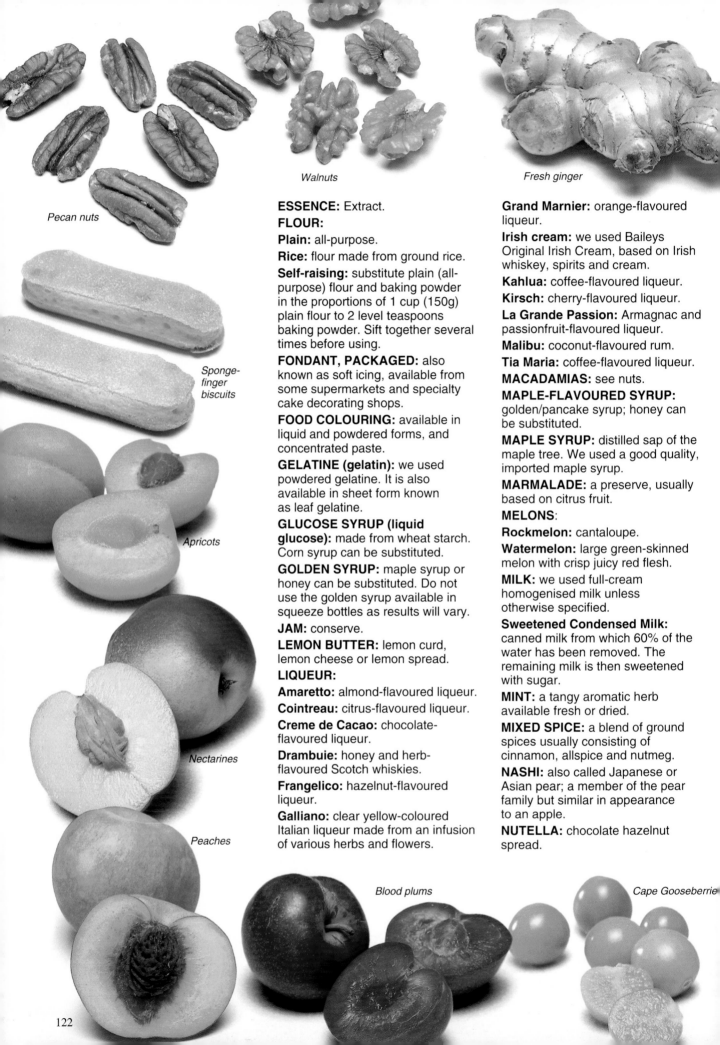

Pecan nuts

Walnuts

Fresh ginger

Sponge-finger biscuits

Apricots

Nectarines

Peaches

Blood plums

Cape Gooseberrie

ESSENCE: Extract.

FLOUR:

Plain: all-purpose.

Rice: flour made from ground rice.

Self-raising: substitute plain (all-purpose) flour and baking powder in the proportions of 1 cup (150g) plain flour to 2 level teaspoons baking powder. Sift together several times before using.

FONDANT, PACKAGED: also known as soft icing, available from some supermarkets and specialty cake decorating shops.

FOOD COLOURING: available in liquid and powdered forms, and concentrated paste.

GELATINE (gelatin): we used powdered gelatine. It is also available in sheet form known as leaf gelatine.

GLUCOSE SYRUP (liquid glucose): made from wheat starch. Corn syrup can be substituted.

GOLDEN SYRUP: maple syrup or honey can be substituted. Do not use the golden syrup available in squeeze bottles as results will vary.

JAM: conserve.

LEMON BUTTER: lemon curd, lemon cheese or lemon spread.

LIQUEUR:

Amaretto: almond-flavoured liqueur.

Cointreau: citrus-flavoured liqueur.

Creme de Cacao: chocolate-flavoured liqueur.

Drambuie: honey and herb-flavoured Scotch whiskies.

Frangelico: hazelnut-flavoured liqueur.

Galliano: clear yellow-coloured Italian liqueur made from an infusion of various herbs and flowers.

Grand Marnier: orange-flavoured liqueur.

Irish cream: we used Baileys Original Irish Cream, based on Irish whiskey, spirits and cream.

Kahlua: coffee-flavoured liqueur.

Kirsch: cherry-flavoured liqueur.

La Grande Passion: Armagnac and passionfruit-flavoured liqueur.

Malibu: coconut-flavoured rum.

Tia Maria: coffee-flavoured liqueur.

MACADAMIAS: see nuts.

MAPLE-FLAVOURED SYRUP: golden/pancake syrup; honey can be substituted.

MAPLE SYRUP: distilled sap of the maple tree. We used a good quality, imported maple syrup.

MARMALADE: a preserve, usually based on citrus fruit.

MELONS:

Rockmelon: cantaloupe.

Watermelon: large green-skinned melon with crisp juicy red flesh.

MILK: we used full-cream homogenised milk unless otherwise specified.

Sweetened Condensed Milk: canned milk from which 60% of the water has been removed. The remaining milk is then sweetened with sugar.

MINT: a tangy aromatic herb available fresh or dried.

MIXED SPICE: a blend of ground spices usually consisting of cinnamon, allspice and nutmeg.

NASHI: also called Japanese or Asian pear; a member of the pear family but similar in appearance to an apple.

NUTELLA: chocolate hazelnut spread.

Vanilla beans

Whole nutmeg

Pine nuts

Whole hazelnuts

Shelled pistachios

Nashis

Dessert nougat

Violet Crumble bars

Kiwi fruit

NUTS:

Macadamia: native to Australia, rich and buttery nut; store in refrigerator because of high oil content.

Pine: also called pignoli; small, cream-coloured kernels obtained from the cones of different varieties of pine trees.

Pistachio: pale green, delicately flavoured nuts inside hard off-white shells. To peel, soak shelled nuts in boiling water for about 5 minutes; drain, then pat dry with absorbent paper. Rub skins with cloth to peel.

OIL:

Macadamia: oil extracted from macadamia nuts.

Olive: a blend of refined and virgin olive oils, good for everyday cooking.

Vegetable: we used a polyunsaturated vegetable oil.

ORANGE FLOWER WATER: concentrated flavouring made from orange blossoms.

PRUNES: whole dried plums.

PUFF PASTRY SHEETS: frozen sheets of puff pastry (measuring 24.5cm square) made from wheat flour; vegetable margarine or butter, salt, food acid and water.

REDCURRANT JELLY: a preserve made from redcurrants.

RICE PAPER: edible sheets of paper made from rice, available from gourmet and Asian food shops.

RIND: zest.

RUM, DARK: we prefer to use an underproof rum (not overproof) for a more subtle flavour.

SAUTERNES-STYLE DESSERT WINE: a white wine made from late-harvested premium grapes; often referred to as a "botrytis-affected" or "sticky" wine.

SEMOLINA: a hard part of the wheat which is sifted out and used mainly for making pasta.

SPONGE-FINGER BISCUITS: also known as Savoiardi, Savoy biscuits or ladyfingers. They are Italian-style, crisp biscuits made from a sponge-cake mixture.

STAR ANISE: the dried star-shaped fruit of an evergreen tree, with an aniseed flavour.

SUGAR: we used coarse granulated table sugar, also known as crystal sugar, unless otherwise specified.

Brown: a soft, fine granulated sugar containing molasses which gives it its characteristic colour.

Caster: fine granulated table sugar; also known as superfine.

Icing sugar mixture: also known as confectioners' sugar or powdered sugar, with the addition of cornflour.

Pure icing: also known as confectioners' sugar or powdered sugar.

SULTANAS: golden raisins.

VANILLA BEAN: dried bean of the vanilla orchid, if used whole it can be used repeatedly. Simply wash in warm water after use, dry well and store in airtight container.

VIOLET CRUMBLE BARS: chocolate-dipped honeycomb; made from chocolate, sugar, glucose and gelatine.

YEAST: 2 level teaspoons (7g) dried yeast is equal to 15g compressed yeast.

Tamarillos

Kumquats

Mangoes

Techniques

Here, we illustrate some of the tricks of the trade which will provide that special finishing touch to many of the recipes featured in this book.

TO REMOVE RIND

Various utensils produce different effects when used to remove rind from oranges, lemons and limes.

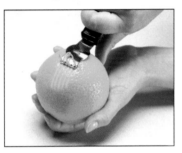

Use a zester on fruit when very fine strips of rind are used as an ingredient in a filling or for a topping.

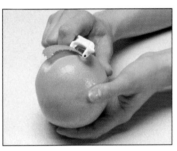

A vegetable peeler will remove citrus rind in wide strips suitable for making candied or glace rind.

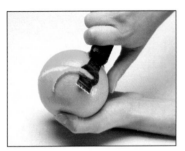

Finer pieces of citrus rind, used when thin strips are to be scattered over a dessert before serving, or in a sugar syrup, can be cut with a canelle knife.

TO TOAST NUTS OR COCONUT

We have used 2 different methods for toasting nuts and coconut.

1: Stir nuts constantly in an ungreased heavy-based frying pan over medium heat until evenly and lightly browned.

2: Spread nuts in a single layer on an oven tray, toast in a moderate oven about 5 to 10 minutes or until lightly browned, stirring occasionally.

Turn toasted nuts immediately onto a heatproof tray, spread out to cool. Store leftover cold nuts in an airtight container in the refrigerator or freezer.

TO MELT CHOCOLATE

● Melt chocolate in a double saucepan or heatproof bowl over a pan of hot water, or stand bowl in sink of hot water or in microwave. Since it scorches easily, it's very important to always melt chocolate slowly.

● Do not allow water to come in contact with chocolate at any time.

● If chocolate turns from a glossy, liquid mass to a dull, coarse-textured consistency, you will have to discard the chocolate and start again.

● To microwave chocolate, break into pieces and spread in a single layer on a microwave-proof plate. Microwave on HIGH until soft. Remember, chocolate still holds most of its shape when melted. The melting time will depend on the oven and the amount to be melted; start checking after 30 seconds.

● Chocolate to be piped can be broken into pieces, placed in a plastic bag (see below) and melted in a microwave oven.

HOW TO MAKE CHOCOLATE CURLS

Using a spatula, spread a thin layer of melted chocolate over a cool surface, such as a large marble or ceramic tile; leave to set at room temperature. Use a large sharp knife, hold it at a 45° angle and pull knife gently over the surface of the chocolate to form curls. Leftover chocolate can be remelted and used again.

USING A PLASTIC BAG AS A PIPING BAG

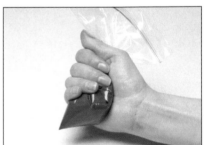

Spoon icing, chocolate or cream into small plastic bag, gently ease down into a corner of the bag, twist the plastic above contents to secure. Snip a tiny hole in one of the bottom corner tips of the bag. Enlarge the hole by snipping away more plastic if necessary. We found that the snap-lock resealable bags by Glad were the strongest variety to use.

MAKING ICE-CREAM BY HAND

Pour the cooled ice-cream mixture into a shallow cake pan. Cover with foil, freeze until just firm then beat ice-cream in a large bowl with electric mixer until just smooth. Return ice-cream to pan, re-cover with foil and freeze until firm.

HOW TO MAKE A PAPER PIPING BAG

Cut a 30cm square of non-stick baking or greaseproof paper in half diagonally.

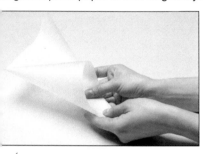

1. Place 1 triangle on the bench with the centre point towards you; curl 1 point under, bringing it towards you until it meets the centre point.

2. Hold these 2 points together with 1 hand, roll remaining point around towards you to meet the other 2 points and form a cone.

3. Tape, fold or staple the cone to hold its shape.

CANNOLI MOULDS

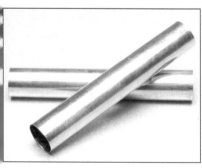

We used cannelloni shells to make cannoli (see page 18) but metal moulds are available in various sizes; those shown are 1.5cm x 10cm.

Index

QUICK CONVERSION GUIDE

Wherever you live in the world you can use our recipes with the help of our easy-to-follow conversions for all your cooking needs. These conversions are approximate only. The difference between the exact and approximate conversion of liquid and dry measures amounts to only a teaspoon or two, and will not make any difference to your cooking results.

MEASURING EQUIPMENT

The difference between measuring cups internationally is minimal within 2 or 3 teaspoons' difference. (For the record, 1 Australian metric measuring cup will hold approximately 250ml.) The most accurate way of measuring dry ingredients is to weigh them. When measuring liquids use a clear glass or plastic jug with the metric markings.

If you would like the measuring cups and spoons as used in our Test Kitchen, turn to page 128 for details and order coupon. In this book we use metric measuring cups and spoons approved by Standards Australia.

- a graduated set of four cups for measuring dry ingredients; the sizes are marked on the cups.
- a graduated set of four spoons for measuring dry and liquid ingredients; the amounts are marked on the spoons.
- 1 TEASPOON: 5ml
- 1 TABLESPOON: 20ml.

NOTE: NZ, CANADA, USA AND UK ALL USE 15ml TABLESPOONS.
ALL CUP AND SPOON MEASUREMENTS ARE LEVEL.

DRY MEASURES

METRIC	IMPERIAL
15g	$1/2$oz
30g	1oz
60g	2oz
90g	3oz
125g	4oz ($1/4$lb)
155g	5oz
185g	6oz
220g	7oz
250g	8oz ($1/2$lb)
280g	9oz
315g	10oz
345g	11oz
375g	12oz ($3/4$lb)
410g	13oz
440g	14oz
470g	15oz
500g	16oz (1lb)
750g	24oz ($1 1/2$lb)
1kg	32oz (2lb)

LIQUID MEASURES

METRIC	IMPERIAL
30ml	1 fluid oz
60ml	2 fluid oz
100ml	3 fluid oz
125ml	4 fluid oz
150ml	5 fluid oz ($1/4$ pint/1 gill)
190ml	6 fluid oz
250ml	8 fluid oz
300ml	10 fluid oz ($1/2$ pint)
500ml	16 fluid oz
600ml	20 fluid oz (1 pint)
1000ml (1 litre)	$1 3/4$ pints

WE USE LARGE EGGS WITH AN AVERAGE WEIGHT OF 60g

HELPFUL MEASURES

METRIC	IMPERIAL
3mm	$1/8$in
6mm	$1/4$in
1cm	$1/2$in
2cm	$3/4$in
2.5cm	1in
5cm	2in
6cm	$2 1/2$in
8cm	3in
10cm	4in
13cm	5in
15cm	6in
18cm	7in
20cm	8in
23cm	9in
25cm	10in
28cm	11in
30cm	12in (1ft)

HOW TO MEASURE

When using the graduated metric measuring cups, it is important to shake the dry ingredients loosely into the required cup. Do not tap the cup on the bench, or pack the ingredients into the cup unless otherwise directed. Level top of cup with knife. When using graduated metric measuring spoons, level top of spoon with knife. When measuring liquids in the jug, place jug on flat surface, check for accuracy at eye level.

OVEN TEMPERATURES

These oven temperatures are only a guide; we've given you the lower degree of heat. Always check the manufacturer's manual.

	C° (Celsius)	F° (Fahrenheit)	Gas Mark
Very slow	120	250	1
Slow	150	300	2
Moderately slow	160	325	3
Moderate	180 - 190	350 - 375	4
Moderately hot	200 - 210	400 - 425	5
Hot	220 - 230	450 - 475	6
Very hot	240 - 250	500 - 525	7

TWO GREAT OFFERS FROM THE AWW HOME LIBRARY

Here's the perfect way to keep your Home Library books in order, clean and within easy reach. More than a dozen books fit into this smart silver grey vinyl folder. PRICE: Australia $11.95; elsewhere $21.95; prices include postage and handling. To order your holder, see the details below.

All recipes in the AWW Home Library are created using Australia's unique system of metric cups and spoons. While it is relatively easy for overseas readers to make any minor conversions required, it is easier still to own this durable set of Australian cups and spoons (photographed). PRICE : Australia: $5.95; New Zealand: $A8.00; elsewhere: $A9.95; prices include postage & handling.
This offer is available in all countries.

TO ORDER YOUR METRIC MEASURING SET OR BOOK HOLDER:
PHONE: Have your credit card details ready. Sydney: (02) 9260 0035; **elsewhere in Australia:** 1800 252 515 (free call, Mon-Fri, 9am-5pm) or FAX your order to (02) 9267 4363 or MAIL your order by photocopying or cutting out and completing the coupon below.
PAYMENT: **Australian residents:** We accept the credit cards listed, money orders and cheques. **Overseas residents:** We accept the credit cards listed, drafts in $A drawn on an Australian bank, also English, New Zealand and U.S. cheques in the currency of the country of issue.
Credit card charges are at the exchange rate current at the time of payment.

Please photocopy and complete coupon and fax or send to:
AWW Home Library Reader Offer, ACP Direct, PO Box 7036, Sydney 1028.

❑ Metric Measuring Set   ❑ Holder

Please indicate number(s) required.

Mr/Mrs/Ms _____

Address _____

_____

Postcode _____ Country_____

Ph: (   ) _____Bus. Hour: _____

I enclose my cheque/money order for $ _____ payable to ACP Direct

OR: please charge my:
❑ Bankcard ❑ Visa ❑ MasterCard ❑ Diners Club ❑ Amex

❑❑❑❑❑❑❑❑❑❑❑❑❑❑❑❑❑❑ Exp. Date ___/__

Cardholder's signature _____

(Please allow up to 30 days for delivery within Australia. Allow up to 6 weeks for overseas deliveries.)

Both offers expire 30/6/97.   AWSF97